CROSSCURRENTS *Modern Critiques*

CROSSCURRENTS *Modern Critiques*
Harry T. Moore, *General Editor*

Contemporary British Novelists

EDITED BY *Charles Shapiro*

WITH A PREFACE BY *Harry T. Moore*

Carbondale and Edwardsville

SOUTHERN ILLINOIS UNIVERSITY PRESS

AS CHARLES SHAPIRO points out in his Introduction to this book, recent spasmodic changes in the British social structure have had an evident effect upon current British writing. The essays in this volume show an awareness of these changes and their effects.

My Preface to an earlier volume in the Cross-currents series, William Van O'Connor's The New University Wits, says virtually all I want to say about these matters, particularly in relation to the historical background of Great Britain today. But there are still some comments that might be made on the individual essays in Mr. Shapiro's book.

The reader will note at once that they are arranged in alphabetical order of authors discussed. Consequently, Kingsley Amis comes first, examined by Ralph Caplan, who finds that Lucky Jim (1954) remains the finest of Amis' novels. Although he has written four since then, he has not grown—if we accept Mr. Caplan's verdict, which is really inescapable. Yet some of Amis' later work is good in spots, particularly Take a Girl Like You (1960), which in tone and situation is reminiscent of various English comic novels of the eighteenth century.

It is in many ways fitting that Amis open this series of discussions, for he is in several ways a pace setter,

and his Jim Dixon has become a somewhat arche-
typal figure. Mr. Caplan believes that Amis is the
"most amusing enemy" of the affectation that threatens the integrity of so much modern writing; we can
only regret that, like so many American writers, as
well as numerous British authors, Amis hasn't grown;
and we can hope that in time he will.

Louis Fraiberg follows with a discussion of Lawrence Durrell's Alexandria Quartet, in which he finds
dissonances, particularly in one of the most important
characters, Justine. Lawrence Durrell has had a strange
career, from the time of his first novel, The Black
Book (1938), his best work of fiction outside the
Quartet. The Black Book had an underground cir-
culation until 1960, that year which saw the fizzling out
of so many of the electrically wired fences of censor-
ship. Meanwhile, in the years after The Black Book,
Durrell had established a minor reputation as an avant-
garde poet. He had begun to achieve fame, particularly
in the United States, England, and France, as the
volumes of the Quartet kept appearing between 1957
and 1960. They bedazzled many readers because the
books were "written" in a time when most fiction was
done in grocery-list prose. Amis, for example, although
he plays with language in light poetry, can't "write";
I use these expressions "write" and "written," in quo-
tation marks, in the sense in which T. S. Eliot employed them in his Introduction, in 1937, to Djuna
Barnes's Nightwood, in which Eliot said the reader
of today isn't used to books that are "written"; and I
use these expressions as Edmund Wilson did, some
years after Eliot, in his essay in which he explained
that he couldn't read Somerset Maugham because
Maugham's books are not "written." Well, Durrell's
are, perhaps at times too much so.

Durrell's reputation has lately suffered somewhat—

Mr. Fraiberg's essay is a symptom of this—because, since the Quartet, he hasn't kept critics and other readers busy with newer novels by him. Durrell has, like Henry James at one period of his career, fallen in love with the theater. His poetic dramas are rather special, perhaps caviare to the general, and have been produced mostly in art theaters in such places as Hamburg or at the Edinburgh Festival. This specialization has kept Durrell out of the eye of the wider public. And critics tend nowadays to dissect the Quartet and look scrupulously for faults in it. This is not to say that Mr. Fraiberg's essay is entirely negative; but he does find those flaws in Justine as a character, particularly developing the point that she is not "interesting" (yet he takes up a great deal of space to show this, which in itself makes her somewhat interesting). Mr. Fraiberg's observation that "mutilation in the Quartet is often the symbol of the way to life" is an acute observation, and one that I don't recall having been made before, at least not so forcefully; and Mr. Fraiberg convincingly develops his point that these novels exemplify "the wound-and-bow theory of creation."

Similarly, Irving Malin gives us some new insights into the work of William Golding, particularly in his discussions of "faulty vision." It is not the novels which in his judgment have faults of vision, but the people in them. This is a theme Mr. Malin continually stresses: in relation to The Lord of the Flies he points out that the stranded boys never really "see" the elemental aspects of their environment, any more than the officer who rescues them can "see" his cruiser or the water that is the element in which it exists. On the other hand, some of the primitive people in Golding's novel don't seem faulty in vision—at least Fa and Nil don't—if only because they think in pictures. But

there is a failure of vision, Mr. Malin points out, in
Tuami, who is one of the future homo sapiens who
are moving in on the Neanderthals, Fa and Nil; like
Tuami, we as readers "cannot see beyond 'the line of
darkness.'" In Pincher Martin, the name character
"cannot marry the elements, or perceive that mind,
body, and essentials are the same 'stuff.'" In Free
Fall, as Mr. Malin points out, Sammy is "wise" only
"when his body—in touch with the many crawling
things—speaks." In The Spire, the sky-loving medieval
dean of a cathedral cannot "see" his own predicament:
"Through his use of the elements, Golding reminds
us that vision hugs the ground."

These are helpful explanations of Golding; in developing them, Mr. Malin makes others. He treats this
author in an almost entirely conceptual way, however;
the question remains as to whether Golding is himself
an important visionary as a creative artist. Are these
settings he creates—wild islands, a primitive world,
a medieval town—artistically authentic evocations, or
are they merely tours de force? My own explorations
of Golding's milieu incline me to believe the latter;
nor have I read anything in the immense amount of
Golding criticism that would convince me otherwise.
But it is good to have Mr. Malin's explanation of
what Golding is trying to do philosophically.

Paul Schlueter immediately stresses the importance
of Doris Lessing, who is of course one of the bright
stars among these authors, with as high a place in the
literary firmament as any of them except perhaps Lawrence Durrell. Mr. Schlueter deals with the often-made
comparison of Mrs. Lessing to Mary McCarthy and
Simone de Beauvoir and, while admitting certain
similarities on the surface, he shows the distinct individuality of Doris Lessing. He presents a full survey
of her career, emphasizing the "Children of Violence"

series and the novel which he designates (rightly, I think) her most important book so far: The Golden Notebook.

Throughout, Mr. Schlueter is concerned with Mrs. Lessing's sense of commitment, her involvement in racial questions during her youth in Africa, leading to her intense socio-political interests. In The Golden Notebook her heroine, apparently somewhat auto-biographical, gets beyond factional orthodoxy but, as Mr. Schlueter indicates, not beyond commitment. I share his hope that the commitment Mrs. Lessing has made to literature itself will be an increasingly fruitful one. Meanwhile we have, in Mr. Schlueter's critical examination of her work, a fine statement as to her present importance as a writer.

In his essay on Iris Murdoch, Leonard Kriegel finds that this author has shown tremendous promise but hasn't yet attained to the stature of a major novelist. Her failure, he notes, is above all a failure of vision. This may seem an odd remark for anyone to make about a writer who was for so long an Oxford don in the area of philosophy—but of course the vision of the teacher of philosophy and that of the creative novelist are altogether different phenomena. Mr. Kriegel substantiates his statement convincingly, though why he should pick the overrated Joyce Cary as a contrast, as a writer who met his artistic problems successfully, is difficult to understand. What is the value of Cary's "vision"? I note that Charles Shapiro, who was given a free hand in his selection of authors to be discussed in this volume, didn't include Cary.

Mr. Kriegel has written a fairly long essay on Iris Murdoch, dealing thoroughly and illuminatingly with all her books. He is continually rooting for her to come through, and he is particularly partial to The Bell, "Miss Murdoch's fourth and finest novel," yet he isn't taken in by her high reputation; he thinks she still really has to make good on the large scale. Mr. Kriegel's criticism of her work is acute, and he has given us some useful perspectives by which to judge it.

Charles Shapiro, in his discussion of Anthony Powell's cycle, "A Dance to the Music of Time," wisely emphasizes the importance of the boorish Kenneth Widmerpool by including his name in the title of the essay. For, in the seven novels that have been published of the proposed twelve, Widmerpool is the dominant figure, in a comically evil way. Mr. Shapiro—who is preparing a volume on Powell for the Crosscurrents series—is somewhat handicapped in the present book because only those seven novels have so far appeared; and yet Mr. Shapiro handles expertly the material at hand. He is not afraid to make a rather bold statement, though the "very well might be" somewhat qualifies it: "Powell very well might be England's best comic writer since Charles Dickens." A good many American readers might disagree, as Mr. Shapiro knows; he points out that Nicholas Jenkins, Powell's narrator, "has a superb, subdued sense of the absurd," and it is just such quiet laughter "which is, at first, a bit alien to American sensibilities," so that it takes American readers a certain amount of time to become attuned to Powell's attitudes and methods. True (and I am not speaking of myself, for on my first reading of the full seven novels of Powell's series, I published a favorable article about them)—and it is particularly difficult to persuade American students to see the virtues in Powell. The difficulty with the classroom approach, of course, is that in most cases only a single novel can be taken up, and readers need to go through at least half a dozen of the books in order to appreciate fully Powell's treatment of the element of time, and his shrewd across-the-years development of his characters. Fortunately, Mr. Shapiro's essay affords an excellent introduction to the cycle as far as it has gone (the seventh volume, as he points out, begins the second half); with him, again stressing the monstrous figure of Widmerpool, "we await developments."

Saul Maloff's study of Alan Sillitoe contains more social background than most of these other essays, if only because Sillitoe so plainly needs just this "placing." Mr. Maloff ignores Sillitoe's most imaginative and least realistic novel, The General, except to dismiss it as this author's poorest work—which it is, his poorest and least typical. Similarly, Mr. Maloff spends very little time with The Key to the Door; he devotes most of his space to Sillitoe's first novel, Saturday Night and Sunday Morning, and to his long story, "The Loneliness of the Long-Distance Runner."

Mr. Maloff expresses some interesting views of Kingsley Amis and John Braine (he doesn't think much of the latter), and makes the valuable observation that Sillitoe doesn't really belong so much to the new group as to the proletarian writers of the 1930's; yet, although atavistic, he is nonetheless a "neo-Marxian." (My Preface to William Van O'Connor's Crosscurrents volume, The New University Wits, contains a comparison between Saturday Night and Sunday Morning and D. H. Lawrence's Sons and Lovers, a comparison based partly on the vocational situation of the hero in each of the novels—they are both workers in Nottingham factories, though in different generations and under quite different conditions). Mr. Maloff makes the extremely interesting point that Sillitoe, although a writer of limited stylistic resources, nevertheless employs a dialect that is not strictly "accurate," but rather "created," and, "for better or worse," a "literary" language.

In his book on C. P. Snow in the Crosscurrents series in 1963, Frederick R. Karl saw Snow "clearly emerging as a major literary figure." In his essay on that author in the present volume, Mr. Karl plays him down. "I have written elsewhere that Snow gives us a sense of how modern man lives. I would strongly qualify that now"—and so on. Since producing his earlier book, Mr. Karl has had a chance to reconsider his views; perhaps his perspectives were somewhat changed as he carefully examined the Victorian and immediately pre-Victorian writers in his excellent study, An Age of Fiction: the Nineteenth-Century British Novel, and as he has worked with the letters which he is editing of an indisputably major novelist— Joseph Conrad. Anyhow, Mr. Karl now finds that C. P. Snow is less interested in people than things; and in attempting to suggest the costive quality of Snow's narrator, Lewis Eliot, Mr. Karl gives literary criticism a somewhat new twist. He also adds an amusing paragraph about the possible effects of President Eisenhower's golf games on world politics. Often when a man who has turned out a book about an author is asked to write a subsequent essay about him, the latter becomes merely a redaction of the former. Not so with Mr. Karl and C. P. Snow; in the light of his book on Snow, the essay Mr. Karl has now written is what, in the old days, we called a blockbuster.

Charles Alva Hoyt gives his essay on Muriel Spark a piquant subtitle, "The Surrealist Jane Austen." The essay doesn't really develop this point, except by indirection; he sees Mrs. Spark as a mischievous writer, not in the sense of one playing tricks on readers, but rather as one who views the universe itself as mischievous. This is a key to the understanding of Mrs. Spark, whose finest books Mr. Hoyt considers Memento Mori and The Prime of Miss Jean Brodie.

He sees her as still a writer of promise rather than of full achievement, and of course this applies to numerous authors who are considered here. But, as Mr. Shapiro says in his Introduction, these writers have "strength and variety"; and certainly this applies to Mrs. Spark, as Mr. Hoyt's essay so convincingly demonstrates.

Among these authors, Angus Wilson alphabetically comes last. Arthur Edelstein has aptly subtitled his critical review of Wilson's career "The Territory Behind," referring to his subject's traditionalism. He makes clear that Wilson is not an innovator and suggests that he "is a novelist more clearly in the line of Henry James than perhaps anyone else writing today." Yes, perhaps; but to hold Angus Wilson up beside Henry James is to show how meager Wilson's talent really is. Yet Mr. Edelstein does make out a good case for Wilson as a writer of subtle motivations, particularly in comparison with Zola, whom he greatly admires. Yet he practices a "delicacy of experiment" beyond Zola's range, "for to the severely limited materials of the Frenchman's laboratory he has added the factor of consciousness as a vital influence upon his characters—and that makes all the difference." Decidedly true; though Mr. Edelstein has to go back to Wilson's Anglo-Saxon Attitudes (1956) to find his "most fully achieved novel so far," and this suggests a lack of growth in Wilson's subsequent work. As Mr. Edelstein further points out, despite Wilson's adeptness at conveying nuances, he "has not yet made an achievement that would place him in the ranks of these great writers," the latter being a number of authors this critic mentions who depend upon the force of their characters' integral development rather than mechanical compromises with coincidence. Yet, as Mr. Edelstein notes, if Wilson sometimes fails even in the realm of interest, his ambition is commendable. Mr. Edelstein evidently enjoys reading Angus Wilson, as many of us do, but that primary point must again be stressed—he is not, like most of the writers considered in this volume, an innovator.

Charles Shapiro has in any event provided us with a fine set of studies of recent British novelists; once again, in terms of his own assertion, they do represent "strength and variety." The commentators he so judiciously selected have been cautious about over-praising the authors they were writing about: from this book we derive the idea that so far none of these writers (except perhaps Lawrence Durrell and Doris Lessing) has produced anything resembling a master-piece. But masterpieces are scarce enough in this age: has there been one in the area of the novel since the Second World War except Thomas Mann's Doktor Faustus (1947)? I think we'll have to wait for a while before making assured statements even about the work of novelists as fine as, say, Albert Camus, Günter Grass, and Saul Bellow. Meanwhile, we have the present-day British novel to consider; in the aggregate it stands up against the French, the German, and the American of these years. The expert examination of the various novelists in this book will show why. Carefully critical, these essays really give us the contemporary British novel.

HARRY T. MOORE

Southern Illinois University
April 23, 1965

RALPH CAPLAN, formerly editor of *Industrial Design*, is a free-lance writer and editor. His essays and poetry have appeared in such publications as the *New Yorker* and the *Nation* and his novel, *Say Yes!* will be published by Doubleday (1965).

LOUIS FRAIBERG, Chairman of the English Department at the University of Toledo, has long been interested in the relationships between psychology and literature. His book on this subject, *Psychoanalysis and American Literary Criticism*, was published in 1960.

IRVING MALIN is the author of two previously published books in the Crosscurrents Series, *New American Gothic* and *Jews and Americans*, as well as a book on William Faulkner. He is a member of the Department of English of the City College of New York.

PAUL SCHLUETER teaches English at Southern Illinois University and is a contributor to *Contemporary American Novelists*. He reviews books for the Christian Century, *Chicago Daily News, Chicago Sun-Times, St. Louis Post-Dispatch*, and the *Denver Post*.

LEONARD KRIEGEL, currently a Fulbright-Mundt lecturer in the Netherlands, is an Assistant Professor of English at City College of New York. He has edited several works of

Mark Twain and has published short stories and his autobiography, *The Long Walk Home* (1964).

CHARLES SHAPIRO, the editor of this volume, is a Professor of English at Briarcliff College. He is the author of *Theodore Dreiser: Our Bitter Patriot* in the Crosscurrents Series, has edited several collections of essays, and has published essays, stories, and poetry in a number of magazines. He is also a regular book reviewer for the *Saturday Review* and the *Louisville Courier-Journal*.

SAUL MALOFF has taught at Bennington College and the universities of Indiana, Iowa, Michigan and Puerto Rico. He is a frequent contributor of criticism and fiction to many publications and is currently Literary Editor of *Newsweek* magazine.

FREDERICK R. KARL is currently working on an edition of the collected letters of Joseph Conrad and teaching at City College of New York. He is the author of a novel, *The Quest*, two books on the English novel, and *C. P. Snow: The Politics of Conscience*.

CHARLES ALVA HOYT, a professional jazz pianist, is on the staff of the English Department of Bennett Junior College. He has published extensively on the Romantic period of English literature in which he has long been interested.

ARTHUR EDELSTEIN teaches English at Hunter College and in 1961–62 held a Stanford Creative Writing Fellowship. His articles and book reviews have been published in the *New Leader, Saturday Review, Jewish Heritage,* and *the New York Post*.

CONTENTS

INTRODUCTION

Charles Shapiro

OUR COLLECTION of essays by American critics on ten important contemporary British novelists is meant to be a tribute to both the strength and variety of British fiction since World War II. It is also an attempt to evaluate and understand the works of individual writers for, unfortunately, American reviewers have tended to be flip when confronted with what is best in British fiction, tossing out terms such as "angry" and "Establishment" to cover up their inability to read and appreciate individual novels. Charges of anglophobia might be raised against these men except for the obvious fact that they are equally obtuse when confronted by works of their own countrymen.

There have been, of course, meaningful changes in postwar England which have been duly observed and interpreted by assorted social-historians, reporters, and special pleaders. While all agree that England is undergoing a rapid democratization and socialization, there has been controversy as to how this has affected the creative life. Obviously young writers have been challenged; men and women who, a generation or so back would have been doomed to gray, pedestrian lives, who would never have dreamed of a university career, are now graduating, teaching, and, best of all, writing. And, unlike their American cousins who rise on the social ladder, they are refusing to accept the values that once kept their fathers from an equal opportunity to develop their potentialities. They see that social upheavals bring about tragedies, and they also seem to be painfully aware of the awkwardness that accompanies a man on his way up. They watch, but at the same time they are part of the change. Others, a bit older and perhaps a bit better placed, have witnessed the new England with less enthusiasm, scorning a "welfare" state which they believe diminishes individual dignity and encourages a lack of respect for tradition.

But while there might be arguments about the politics and economics of Britain today, it is evident that the social reorganization has made for the very stuff of fiction, and, in their various ways many writers have responded to the changes about them, and they have created a lively literature.

Exciting things have also been occurring in American fiction, but while in England the action seems to often come from the facts of the lessening of class differences, in America the strength comes from a different set of social forces—the more than gradual emergence of the Jewish intellectual to the heart of the literary community and the fierce struggle of the Negro-American to be part of his country. Most of the important work in fiction in America is being done by members of these two minority groups, and as a result American fiction is more furious, wide-swinging, and dangerous. If we must speak of "angry" writers at all, they are American writers, not British, coming from the same lonely tradition which produced such alienated men as Ahab and Joe Christmas. There is, at present, no British equivalent to our "Invisible Man" or Herzog.

English writers, as Walter Allen has observed, do

not suffer as we do from a deep sense of alienation. Perhaps this is the reason for their consistent and artful use of comedy, for a sense of the comic in us all that we fail to match. As one critic puts it, "The British comic tradition is one expressive of a confidence that horrors can be handled." Contemporary British novelists have been especially adept at ridicule; they understand suffering but never forget social absurdities. In any case, they write well, and they have a good deal to tell us.

EACH CONTRIBUTOR to this volume was given complete freedom to discuss, damn, or commend as he wished. We are only bound together in this eclectic volume by our sense of the value of the books we write about. There are, of course, many novelists we might have included. The works of such men as William Cooper, John Wain, and a special favorite of mine, G. W. Target deserve careful reading and much praise. It is hoped that English readers of this book will not find us too presumptuous; we are writing out of love, out of a desire to communicate our enthusiasm for an exciting literature.

Ossining, New York
April 12, 1965

Contemporary British Novelists

KINGSLEY AMIS

Ralph Caplan

Whatever happened to Lucky Jim? He got fat. That's the
answer Kingsley Amis gives us ten years and four novels on.

THAT OBSERVATION from the *Birmingham Post* (England?
Michigan? Alabama?) appears on the dust jacket of the
American edition of *One Fat Englishman*, Kingsley Amis'
most recent novel.

It might be interesting to try out the same approach on
other novelists. Whatever happened to Philip Carey? He
went Asiatic. Whatever happened to Jake Barnes? He got
old. Whatever happened to Augie March? He became a
compulsive pen pal.

Dust jacket copy is, of course, privileged material, and
the rules of the game have never required that it mean
anything. Yet that curious quote, ripped from whatever
context, does mean something. It reminds us that Kingsley
Amis, novelist, poet, short story writer, science fiction editor, and interpreter, is still known to the world at large
(including all three Birminghams) as the author of *Lucky
Jim*.

Well why not? It is far and away the best of his five
novels. This is not the customary carping at a novelist for
not-having-lived-up-to-the-promise. . . . *Lucky Jim* never
promised anything more than unmitigated pleasure and
insight, and these it keeps on delivering. The book was not

promise but fulfillment, a commodity we confront too seldom to know how to behave when it is achieved. This seems to be true particularly when the achievement is comic. Have we forgotten how to take humor straight? Unable to exit laughing, the contemporary reader looks over his shoulder for Something More. The trouble is that by now he knows how to find it. So Amis' prodigious gifts were regarded from the first as instrumental, a kit for exploring social problems, and fairly restricted social problems at that.

I first heard about *Lucky Jim* from a young Englishman who praised it wholly in terms of the red-brick university and England's undistributed middle class. It was, he explained soberly, satire directed at a kind of university atmosphere no American could be expected to understand. (At the time we were both standing on the campus of an American university that, in every major respect, could have served as a model for the one in the book.) What he did not say, what he seemed not to have noticed or thought worth mentioning, was that it is *funny*.

But that is precisely what matters. Kingsley Amis, writing of Peter De Vries, speaks of "how funny, and hence how serious, the stuff is," observing that "the gaiety of the whole performance evinces a rare skill and integrity. This is what the satirist works toward and seldom achieves." *Lucky Jim*, like *Comfort Me With Apples*, does achieve it, but the performance—and it *is* a performance—is best appreciated by acknowledging the order: how funny, and *hence* how serious.

For reference, let's recall Amis' novels and some of their themes. In order of publication:

Lucky Jim—Jim Dixon, a misplaced university lecturer, is threatened with losing his job through bad luck, through his own ineptitude, through enemies he is unlucky and inept enough to make. In the end he does lose his job, and shakes free of his girl, but gets a better job and a better girl. Rage at phoniness, rage at sexual deprivation, rage at injustice.

I Like it Here—Garnet Bowen, a non-writing novelist, finds himself doing something he loathes and fears: going abroad. After a brief period in Portugal, he loses some prejudices, strengthens others, changes not at all. Rage at phoniness, insecurity of being abroad ("he fancied that he had a long history of lower-middle-class envy directed against the upper-middle-class traveler who handled foreign railway-officials with insolent ease, discussed the political situation with the taxi-driver in fluent *argot*, and landed up first go at exactly the right hotel.")

That Uncertain Feeling—John Lewis is a bright, lazy, book-bored assistant librarian caught up in the spinning of the big wheels in a small Welsh town. He is taken up by Elizabeth Gruffyd-Williams, wealthy leader of the town's jet set, and shuttles between the fast life and the incredibly mean furnished-apartment existence he shares with his wife and children. He is up for a promotion at the library and an affair with Mrs. Gruffyd-Williams, escapes both, and when last seen is running from a blonde. Rage at boredom, rage at phoniness, rage at meanness of life.

Take a Girl Like You—Jennie Bunn is a sexy, good natured virgin who holds on to her virginity in the face of what seem to be, and finally prove to be, unbeatable odds. Rage at sexual deprivation, rage at phoniness (in neither case on the part of the heroine).

One Fat Englishman—Roger Micheldene is a very fat, selfish, greedy, highly prejudiced Englishman who comes to America in pursuit of his Danish ex-mistress, and gets put in his place by a crazy young Jewish novelist, and by almost everyone else. Rage at America, rage at sexual deprivation, rage at things as they are, however they are.

The outrageous oversimplifications above show how dangerous it is to think of Amis in terms of what he is telling, rather than of how he is telling it. His endowments include a ridiculously accurate ear, an eye that, like those in old samurai movies, misses nothing, and a deadly comic aim. He notices things about us, and humor is the medium for sharing what he notices.

For example, near the end of *Lucky Jim* Dixon has to get to the railroad station before Christine's train leaves. After a "lung-igniting" sprint, he catches the station bus, which, however, is following a lorry-with-trailer along a winding road.

> They entered a long stretch of straight road, with a slight dip in the middle so that every yard of its empty surface was visible. Far ahead an emaciated brown hand appeared from the lorry's cab and made a writhing, beckoning movement. The driver of the bus ignored this invitation in favour of drawing to a gradual halt by a bus stop. . . . The foreshortened bulks of two old women . . . waited until the bus was quenched of all motion before clutching each other and edging with sidelong caution . . . towards the platform. In a moment he heard their voices crying unintelligibly to the conductor, then activity seemed to cease. At least five seconds passed; Dixon stirred elaborately at his post, then twisted himself about looking for anything that might have had a share in causing this caesura in his journey. . . . Was the driver slumped in his seat, the victim of syncope, or had he suddenly got an idea for a poem? . . . the picture of sleepy rustic calm was modified by the fairly sudden emergence from a cottage some yards beyond of a third woman . . . [who] approached with a kind of bowed shuffle that suggested the movements of a serviceman towards the pay table.
>   . . . Dixon found that his whole being had become centered in the matter of the bus's progress; he couldn't be bothered any longer to wonder what Christine would

say to him if he got there in time, nor what he'd do if he
didn't. He just sat there . . . stretching his face in a fresh
direction at each overtaking car, each bend, each motive-
less circumspection of the driver.

The bus was now resolutely secured again behind the
trailer, which soon began to reduce speed even further.
Before Dixon could cry out . . . the lorry and trailer had
moved off to the side into a lay-by and the bus was travelling
on alone. Now was the time, he thought with reviving
hope, for the driver to start making up some of the time he
must have lost. The driver, however, was clearly unable
to assent to this diagnosis . . .

As the traffic thickened slightly towards the town, the
driver added to his hypertrophied caution a psychopathic
devotion to the interests of other road users; the sight of
anything between a removal van and a junior bicycle
halved his speed to four miles an hour. . . . Learners
practised reversing across his path; gossiping knots of
loungers parted leisurely at the touch of his reluctant bon-
net; toddlers reeled to relieve toys from under his just-
revolving wheels. Dixon's head switched angrily to and fro
in vain search for a clock.

I have quoted at length from an admittedly minor scene,
one which illuminates none of the shifting values Kingsley
Amis is celebrated for revealing, because it is in such scenes
that Amis is often most rewarding. Like W. C. Fields he is
able to make us laugh at frustration at the very time he
makes us share the anguish of it. Nor is this particular
scene merely isolated comedy. It is an expression of the
pace and circumstance of Dixon's life.

Largely because so much of it is told from Jenny's point
of view, *Take a Girl Like You* has relatively little of that
kind of thing, and it is the book I find least convincing in
all respects, as if in relinquishing his comic rights Amis had
also sacrificed his right to be taken seriously. This, ironically, is the book in which his intention appears most
earnest: to explore the values behind the strategy in the
war between men and women. Jenny Bunn, however, is
really a *goyishke* Marjorie Morningstar, whom she re-

sembles in her dullness, her stock prettiness, and her earnest, unceasing perception of everything about what men want except why they want it. Like Marjorie, Jenny has nothing to commend her but beauty, candor, and an unruptured hymen. And, like Marjorie, she loses one of them along the way and regrets it. Amis does succeed, in this novel, in "getting into a girl's mind." But getting into Jenny Bunn's mind is like getting into one of Dr. Norman Vincent Peale's popular Sunday morning services: once you are in, the joke is entirely on you.

While *Take a Girl Like You* is a novel about sex, the sex in it is pretty much devoid of excitement. Amis characters generally feel sexually deprived. Actually, they make a lot of contact, one way or another, but are rarely transported by it. Fat Roger, methodically choosing between a martini or a roll on the grass with Mrs. Atkins; John Lewis kissing Elizabeth; Graham kissing Jenny or Julian kissing Jenny or Dick kissing Jenny or Patrick kissing Jenny or Tony kissing Jenny or, for that matter, Anna kissing Jenny; Bowen kissing Emilia—these adventures seldom provoke any response more impassioned than, "That was nice, wasn't it?" Although their response to sexual experience is blander than can be explained wholly in terms of national stereotype, the men in Amis do run across an astonishing abundance of easy lays. Even Roger Micheldene has an experienced and acceptable nymphomaniac constantly at his disposal, and he does manage to get to bed with Helene, the gorgeous Dane. That's not bad for a man who is physically revolting and only lately heterosexual.

The most interesting sex relationships in these books are unconsummated, or at least inactive: Dixon's feeling for Christine, the Dixon-Margaret syndrome (a masterpiece), the frayed marriage in *That Uncertain Feeling*, the dreary, barren, Dickless Martha in *Take a Girl Like You*. Perhaps this is because sexual release runs counter to the world Amis keeps showing us—a world of outs rather than ins, a world in which the outs can neither lick them nor join them. Having no very strong drives toward success in any sense, the Amis hero is not in the traditional position of pressing his nose against a windowpane; rather he finds that someone is always shoving a windowpane up to his nose. The resultant rage is never sexually discharged.

It is usually not discharged overtly at all. The Amis protagonist does not suffer fools gladly. In fact, a good deal of his energy goes into wishing violence on them. He wants to kick them, smash them, push buildings over on them. But what he does instead is to fantasize, and Amis' unique creative powers are nowhere more impressive than in these fantasies. In Jim Dixon's sanity-saving array of faces there is enough inventive genius to sustain a dozen comic novels. (The more extroverted characters, too, blaze on the inside; even Roger Micheldene lives an inner life of fury unsuspected by those who see only his surface nastiness).

While the Amis hero is likely to be anti-intellectual, he is always cerebral. Unlike the Romantic hero who feels when everyone else is busy thinking and knowing, he sees when everyone else is busy feeling and pretending to think. It is what he sees that drives him to rage. But the rage is itself a function of his insight. Instead of being blinded by rage, Amis' characters are able to see clearly by its light. Anger is an instrument of revelation. And of self-revelation.

The enraged perceptions in Amis' fiction are universally valid, which is why the critical class labels have so little to do with what his novels really communicate. *Understand* Margaret Peel? Is there a graduate student anywhere in America who hasn't *dated* her? As for Professor Welch, it is the fact that he is so concretely realized that makes his ubiquity convincing. He is the comfortable fraud, the obtusely well meaning fraud, the fraud as organized and protected by society.

For the phoney is what Kingsley Amis is attacking,

although that term so dear to American writers does not often appear in his books. *Lucky Jim* is set against the entrenchment of the spurious: the university is a fake; the revival of folk art is a fake; Merrie England was a fake, and Margaret's calling it "the Middle Age" is a fake; Bertrand is sham incarnate.

There is nothing unusual about a satirical novel in which the main character finds himself surrounded by fakes. But *Lucky Jim* is a novel whose protagonist is, himself, a fake in the context in which he must move. Dixon is as upset and indignant at his own lack of authenticity as at anyone else's, and as amusing in perceiving it. When, for example, having to give a seminar in "Medieval Life and Culture," he is asked by a prospective member what the course will cover, Dixon replies:

> "I thought I might start with a discussion of the university . . . in its social role." He comforted himself for having said this by the thought that at least he knew it didn't mean anything.

> "You don't propose to offer an analysis of scholasticism, then, I take it?"

> This question illustrated exactly why Dixon felt he had to keep Michie out of his subject. Michie knew a lot, or seemed to, which was as bad. One of the things he knew, or seemed to, was what scholasticism was. Dixon read, heard, and even used the word a dozen times a day without knowing, though he seemed to. But he saw clearly that he wouldn't be able to go on seeming to know the meaning of this and a hundred such words while Michie was there questioning, discussing, and arguing about them.

This, however, is not to say that he cannot acknowledge the genuine, and long for a world in which it might flourish, and he share it. Walking across the lawn with Welch, Dixon reflects that he and the professor must look donnish to students passing by:

> He and Welch might well be talking about history, and in the way history might be talked about in Oxford and

Cambridge quadrangles. At moments like this Dixon came near to wishing that they were really were.

Spiritually speaking Jim Dixon is, like Alfred Doolittle, one of the undeserving poor. He *is* lucky, ending up with the girl, the job, the triumph over all his adversaries, the freedom from Margaret and from the guilt that freedom from Margaret might have been expected to mean. He deserves none of it — except negatively, since Bertrand, who would otherwise triumph, deserves victory even less and is an insufferable bastard besides. As far as the job goes, Gore-Urquardt, who gives it to him, reminds Dixon: "It's not that you've got the qualifications, for this or any other work, but there are plenty who have. You haven't got the disqualifications, though, and that's much rarer."

Amis heroes are, by and large, "not disqualified," rather than positively qualified, for their jobs and for life generally. Librarian John Lewis is not much interested in books or library, but he is about as suitable for the job he seeks as anyone else around, and it is as suitable for him as any other job might be. Writer Garnet Bowen is an indifferent critic and teacher, a supposed novelist temporarily become a supposed playwright. Writing and writers bore him, and Amis produces some marvelously boring examples of each to make the point. Roger Micheldene is apparently an astute enough publisher, but his personal motives get in the way of his business judgment; and reading bores him as much as writing bores Bowen.

Mary McCarthy, discussing the disappearance of character from modern fiction, asserts that "only two names in recent fiction have 'stuck': Gulley Jimson (Joyce Cary) and Lucky Jim (Kingsley Amis). . . ." One thinks immediately of others — Lolita, James Bond, Barry Goldwater — but certainly it is true that Jim Dixon and some other Amis heroes are "characters" in an old fashioned sense. For one thing, they have been exaggerated into believability. For another, they are surrounded at every turn with credible minor characters. Amis is a master of the bit part, the instant characterization. His economy is sometimes almost literally stunning—one remembers large scenes in which character is developed, and finds upon checking that they come down to nothing more than the university instructor pulling out "the curved nickel-banded pipe round which he was trying to train his personality, like a creeper up a trellis."

The novels are old fashioned in another sense: they are written along what seem like conventional lines. Our funniest serious writers operate in spheres where—as in space—the old natural laws need not confine them. Heller's *Catch 22*, Blechman's *How Much?*, Friedman's *Stern*, and Stern's *Golk* all take place in such wild narrative regions, and in fact the novelist in *One Fat Englishman* has written a satire on the blind, called *Blinkie Heaven*, that would be at home in the same locales. But Amis' own instincts run toward a sort of anti-social realism. This is deceptive: while the characters ostensibly live on fictionally familiar streets, they inhabit fantasy worlds as crazily compelling as that of Walter Mitty—or of each of us.

The situations in which these characters appear are propelled by a story sense so strong that one occasionally feels that Amis' plotting power is too much for the slight tale it has to carry, just as, in the forties, Ford cars were thought to have engines too strong for the chassis. The sense of story carries over even into character, and at the end of a novel, the protagonist is likely to share the feeling that it *is* the end. (e.g., When Welch's second son finally appears, Dixon recognizes that he has come "on stage at last just as the curtain was about to ring down.")

For all his sense of story, though, Amis is remarkably self-indulgent. He can afford to be. Most often this takes the form of verbal play: "My daughter Eira (for it was she) went on calling me (for it was me). . . ." Sometimes he uses in one novel a piece of dialogue that has done service in an earlier one—not, I believe, a matter of the *New Yorker's* in-love-with-the-sound-of-one's-own-words, but simply because it has worked once, and does again: "How much did you have?" "Oh, I never count them. It's a bad habit, is counting them." (*Lucky Jim*) "How many have you had, do you think, about?" "Oh, I never count them. It's a bad habit, counting them." (*Take a Girl Like You*) Very frequently he repeats the device of turning what someone has said into a transitional interior pun (". . . *you've really got to hand it to her.* . . . Bowen conducted a brief inner debate on the topic of what he would most like to hand Mrs. Knowles . . ."). Or the inside joke of L. S. Caton, narratively important in *Lucky Jim*, who keeps popping up in other novels, always having "announced without formality on a sheet of paper hastily torn from a pad, bearing a few lines ill-written in green ink that he is on his way to, or from, Latin America, and will be writing again in due course."

Actually, the entire resolution of *Lucky Jim* is gratuitous. It is signaled by a very early scene in which Dixon, standing in a badly lighted pub men's room, experiences a poignantly painful image of a London he doesn't know, and a feeling that someone he has not yet met is about to come into the room. It is further signaled, technically, by Gore-Urquardt's mysterious interest in him, Christine's half hearted, but equally mysterious, interest in him, and a conviction shared by all hands that Bertrand has got to get his if the world makes any sense at all. But it *doesn't* make sense at all, or hasn't so far; and the novel comes to a false climax in which Dixon gives in to life as it is (or as it has been and promises to go on being), and all when he has another kind of life in his grasp.

Margaret comes to his room to make a scene. Normally he puts up with these, but this time he is tired and angry enough to tell her to pack it up. She has a fit of hysterics, and after coming out of it has a temporary moment of truth in which she gives Dixon an opening for declaring the relationship over. He takes it. But as soon as she leaves he feels guilty, and the following day, heavy with the weight of pity and resignation, he tells Margaret that, because of her, he is giving up Christine. She says: " 'Don't be ridiculous. You'd have much more fun with her than you ever had with me.' 'That's as may be. The point is that I've got to stick to you.' He said this without bitterness, nor did he feel any."

The book could very well end somewhere around there, and be true to life as Amis has shown us life. We could take it all right, but he can't; or, rather, doesn't wish to. No, he produces Catchpole, a character hidden since the beginning of the second chapter, to spring Dixon with a baffling irrelevant elaboration of plot. Who needs it? Not the reader. Not Dixon, who had his chance and gave it up and who could easily have guessed most of what Catchpole told him, and in any case had been given the same advice long ago by Carol Goldsmith. As Amis characters in all five novels keep asking about any social oddity, Why? *Why?*

No reason, except that Amis wants it that way, just as there is no reason for everyone in *The Sun Also Rises* to detest Cohn, except that Hemingway does. Dixon's flood of fortune seems almost a reward bestowed on him by Amis for his performance at the evening lecture, one of the most imaginative and comic scenes in modern fiction. What reader could begrudge Dixon anything after that?

Describing Richard Nixon's presidential campaign supporters, Murray Kempton says they were "the very boys who gird up the kidneys for a week and then call the cutest girl in the class and she says she has a date for tomorrow and tomorrow and tomorrow. . . . Richard Nixon is the candidate of all those who had pimples when they were young."

Well, Dixon is the candidate of all those who know that
Homecoming Queens are not for them; but who know too
that no one else is as well equipped to appreciate Homecoming Queens; who know further that those who get the
Homecoming Queens are, by definition, never worth coming home to. (Graham, in *Take a Girl Like You,* is a sort
of unlucky Jim.) Dixon's first view of Christine makes the
point:

> The sight of her seemed an irresistible attack on his
> own habits, standards, and ambitions. Something designed
> to put him in his place for good. The notion that women
> like this were never on view except as the property of men
> like Bertrand was so familiar to him that it had long since
> ceased to appear an injustice. The huge class that con-
> tained Margaret was destined to provide his own women-
> folk.

That Dixon nevertheless gets the girl is not preposterous.
(Nixon, after all, nearly won the election.) But it is unaccountable. Except by luck:

> To write things down as luck wasn't the same as writing
> them off as nonexistent or in some way beneath considera-
> tion. Christine was still nicer and prettier than Margaret,
> and all the deductions that could be drawn from that fact
> should be drawn: there was no end to the ways in which
> nice things are nicer than nasty ones. It had been luck, too,
> that had freed him from pity's adhesive plaster.

Maybe it's luck too that brings us Kingsley Amis at a
time when the integrity of so much of our writing is
threatened by affectation. He is its most amusing enemy.

DURRELL'S DISSONANT QUARTET

Louis Fraiberg

THERE ARE INTERESTING characters in the *Alexandria Quartet*, but Justine is not one of them. Her beauty, intelligence, attractiveness, and what in another might have become her drama, are all negated by the engulfing emptiness which is to be found at her center. And this is appropriate since she is the prototype and symbol of the malaise which Lawrence Durrell depicts as the affliction of modern man. This dis-ease arises from the impossibility of attaining wholeness as a person, and the book is an account of some of the different ways in which wholeness, and therefore fulfillment, is sought by the Alexandrians. Justine is the most outstandingly unsuccessful of them all.

The search is conducted by two classes of people, ordinary—if we may call any of the characters in this novel ordinary—and gifted. The former seek their salvation through sex, the latter through art. Durrell himself says the book is an investigation of modern love, and this is true as far as it goes, for the physical act of sex is seen by his characters as the key to reality and therefore to the possibility of becoming whole by entering into a right relationship with the world as it is. It is my thesis that it fails them and that the ones who come closest to finding the real reality are those whose vocation provides them with quite a different key: pain through mutilation and the knowledge of death. Durrell appears to lose sight of his original intention and, as the *Quartet* progresses, his focus shifts to the artist as seer. The mere lovers are left to discover for themselves how futile love is.

In Durrell's view the intelligible world has suffered a loss of the values which create selfhood and has precipitated us into a desperate attempt to replace them. His characters thus are existentialists trying to become transcendentalists in order that they may become existentialists once more. They are looking for a glimpse of the heraldic universe, the abode of truth, and their method is the compulsive immersion in a bath of experience, the experience of art, of politics, of war, of love.

It is a bath rather than a crucible because the immersion is passive, a watching to see what will happen rather than a testing of the potentialities of the self when challenged. The trouble is that, by Durrell's definition, most of them have no self, and this lack is what frustrates if it does not precisely doom them. It makes them incapable of tragedy, incapable of feeling, and capable only of suffering pain. It sends them on a search for something strong enough to penetrate their defensive shells and make up for what is missing within, even at the cost of suffering. They hope this will prove to them that the world is real and that they do not merely exist but actually live in it.

A measure of how slim their chances are is the clumsiness which they display in the quest. They seem to try out nearly all the possible love relationships in a parody of the method of the social scientists. It is as though a great chart has been drawn up showing the various ways in which A and B and C can impinge upon each other and that then each of them sets out systematically to test as many as lie within his power [perhaps capacity is a better word]. And the parody is developed still further by the relentless analysis to which each experimental coupling is subjected before, during, and after the act. These directly shared introspections are supplemented by related insights occurring in conversations with others, in letters, or, notably, in excerpts from Arnauti's novel, *Moeurs,* and in Pursewarden's notebook. The great preoccupation is hardly ever out of their minds, and it furnishes an important part of the texture of the entire *Quartet,* so important that many readers take it for the essence of the book.

The gradual revelation of Justine as lover dominates this aspect of the *Quartet,* though it may not be immediately apparent on a first reading since there is such a bewildering succession of other lovers and such kaleidoscopic shifts of place, focus, and tempo. But it is possible to see her character from outside the novel, as it were, by unifying along realistic lines some of the elements of Durrell's prismatic technique. What we get then is an impression which corresponds to the *gestalten* we receive through seeing people in a series of unrelated situations. In both instances, though the mosaic is far from complete, there is enough of it to establish a coherent configuration. Justine is then revealed to us as a character of a more familiar kind than we were aware of while under the spell of Alexandria, though—or perhaps because—this process divests her of considerable exoticism and surprise.

Justine—that "tiresome old sexual turnstile through which presumably we must all pass," as Pursewarden resignedly calls her—is the key to the first level on which the *Quartet* may be read. Here are displayed the author's expressly stated intentions toward his creations. In the words of Pursewarden again:

> You see, Justine, I believe that Gods are men and men Gods; they intrude on each other's lives, trying to express themselves through each other. . . . And then (listen) I think that very few people realize that sex is a psychic and not a physical act. The clumsy coupling of human beings is simply a biological paraphrase of this truth—a primitive method of introducing minds to each other, engaging them.

Its psychic quality is to him a reality which is accessible to scrutiny by the mind and not a mystique whose ultimate significance is derived from an experience that bypasses intellection altogether.

It is interesting to look at Justine from this point of view by reconstructing the narrative line and recapitulating her own passing through the turnstiles of other loves. Despite the "many others" who achieve only incidental mention as her early lovers and despite some uncertainty as to chronological sequence left by our threading the maze in this mirror-house of a *Quartet*, a more or less consistent pattern emerges. That is, if Justine were to appear as a character in another novel, one in which time were treated in the familiar way, we should immediately recognize her.

Her background is obscure. We learn that the most important event in her early life has been Capodistria's rape of her as a child; we are not told at what age. The resulting trauma has produced what she calls The Check, a massive inhibition which makes it impossible for her to love freely and which impels her to devote herself to a persistent search for a cure. This is not the sole explanation of her motives—Durrell is careful to reject such oversimplification—it is not even the genesis of them. She is obviously one of those whose disposition is not ardent, though she tries mightily to act with passion. When she succeeds, it is only temporarily and only in a specific constellation of circumstances that happens to appeal to certain sides of her nature. When the external situation changes, she subsides once more into her normally less intense state. Through innate passivity, through the unstated influences of her upbringing, and through the crystallizing effect of the childhood rape, she has been driven back upon herself, only to find there that she cannot feel. In flight from this emotional vacuum she reaches out toward the world of love in hope of finding in it a talisman that will stir her into life. Intuitively recognizing her lack of inner resources, she seeks rescue by some external agency. Justine's love-life which follows from this is the paradigm of the human condition as Durrell portrays it and as he causes it to be explained by Pursewarden.

It is not the "clumsy coupling" of bodies that is at the center of this book, even though its depiction and consequences occupy most of the space and even though Durrell himself advertises the *Quartet* as an investigation of modern love, which most readers take to mean physical sexual encounters. As Pursewarden's remark shows, the psychic significance of the act is the key. And throughout Justine's adventures—throughout the meaningful events in the lives of all the other characters—what matters most is the egocentric, isolated position of the individual and his amoral attempt to use the rest of the world for his own rescue. This is the way Durrell depicts love. Through seemingly countless demonstrations it is made clear that, in the *Quartet*, love is self-love and furthermore that it is a failure.

Justine proves this again and again in her curiously joyless loves. Her marriage to Arnauti fails in part because he does not recognize that her lack of affect is constitutional and that her attempts to acquire some are, to say the least, ambivalent. In his relentless amateur psychologizing he misses the point and so dooms his effort to cure Justine of The Check and win all her love for himself.

She has suffered a loss which Arnauti apparently ignores; it is nowhere indicated that he deals with it or even that he understands its meaning to her. This is the disappearance of her child, and she responds to it as though it were the loss of part of her body. When this is superimposed upon her natural gelidity—thus connecting the generalized shock with an object which, besides having a meaning of its own, also unconsciously represents the organs of loving—it is as though she has accepted defeat and will henceforth be governed by the need to defend herself against the danger of feeling once more. Arnauti's bungling attacks on her defenses against affect can serve only to alienate her from him, and this is what happens. He loses the case.

The "affair" with Clea also exhibits some of the aspects of narcissism. It is more or less passive on Justine's part; apparently it was Clea who initiated it and who finally broke it off. Justine appears to have accepted it temporarily because its inherent sterility was well suited to her temperament. Clea was using her for her own purposes—artistic ones, as it turned out—and both women gained something from the fact that the relationship was based on exhibitionism. For Clea, Justine was a model whose intriguing exterior promised the unraveling of a mystery. Only later did she discover that the beautiful mask concealed a blankness. For Justine, the display of her beauty, her visible body, was enough. There being little within, she obtained such pleasure as she could from her external appearance. Her deadened affective life and Clea's distraction by other interests combined to make the "affair" a pallid one. Justine seems to have accepted its termination with equanimity and to have retained her friendship with Clea.

She had much better luck with Pursewarden. His refusal to let her dominate him enabled her to nourish the comforting illusion that she could have experienced real love if only he had been willing to accept her on her terms. But he sensibly refused to let her take him seriously, and—this proved to be a touch of genius—"discovered to her the fact that she was ridiculous." It was his naturalness, forthrightness, and humor that brought this about, and these qualities, so irresistible to her, were paradoxically the very ones that made it impossible for her to capture him. His devotion to the physical realities of life and his conviction of their moral worth—again paradoxically, they seem to have been among the compelling reasons for his suicide—went far to help her overcome the worst effects of The Check.

Their first love-making came as a result of his conquest of her "by impudence," as Balthazar remarked. In the course of it she was induced to laugh at him and even at herself a little. But it was the fact that he was "utterly himself in a curious way" which aroused in her "an unfamiliar passionate curiosity," another instance of her inability to feel passion except in some way extraneous to love itself even while she was reaching out toward what was genuine in him.

At this point Pursewarden pulled his brilliant psychological coup. He attacked the image of Claudia in *Moeurs*, which Justine had adopted as part of a comforting defensive pattern of self-pity, making it unnecessary for her to face the psychic truth about herself. He simply refused to regard her as a case, as the misguided Arnauti had done, and told her bluntly that she had in all probability tacitly invited the rape by Capodistria and that moreover she had almost certainly enjoyed it, upon which the conquest by impudence became something much more valuable to her: therapy by insult. Pursewarden's heavyhandedness furnished enough of a shock at last to breach this particular defense, and it succeeded because she was sufficiently attached to him to accept it. His motives, too, were different from Arnauti's since he was not seeking personal gain. By keeping himself impregnable to her ardors he was thus able to administer the first check to The Check.

With the same heavyhandedness, again made possible by what may be called the therapeutic nature of their relationship, he conceived the idea of making her go back to the brothel where her child had died. She went willingly, outwardly cool and composed. She had been incapable of acknowledging the child's death and had tried to maintain the illusion that it had simply been lost so that she could continue to live for the sake of searching for it. Now, through Pursewarden's mediation, she entered the room, lay upon the old divan which had become for her the symbol of her loss, and stroked it "with a calm, voluptuous gesture" as though finally reconciling herself to the reality of death by a symbolic act of mothering. When soon afterward the child prostitutes swarmed into the room, she won them over with another motherly act, telling them a story—the story of the "great many petalled love" of Yuna and Aziz! Completely hers now that they had been treated as little children, "They said farewell in voices of heartbreaking sweetness," and she took her departure, emotionally exhausted.

Thereafter she appeared to be almost completely free of the effects of the rape and the death of her child, although her native lack of ardor still prevented her from attaining the full satisfaction of love. When she returned to Nessim and to the marriage which both acknowledged to be without love, she was able to bring passion to it only in response to his invitation to share the dangers of the Palestine plot in which he was one of the leaders. Its failure, resulting in Nessim's political impotence and physical wounding in an air raid—he lost a finger and an eye—destroyed the basis for their renewed intimacy and transformed their desperately contrived semblance of love into its opposite. When Darley visited Justine following these events, she had turned into a sullen, irascible virago who could only hate Nessim and whose conversation with him was limited almost entirely to insult, recrimination, and loathing.

Her renaissance at the end of the fourth book is reported by Clea to be connected with "something much bigger this time." She is apparently reconciled with Nessim on pretty much the old terms, evidently because he is essentially repeating his former role. And she is radiant, her eyes sparkling with delight at her ascendancy over the toad-like Memlik who had previously been such a menace to them both. This is Justine in her element. Clea writes Darley: "It was as if, like some powerful engine of destruction, she had suddenly switched on again. She has never looked happier or younger." The passion which is presumably once more possible for her is passion in the service of the externally induced political excitement, not love.

Justine is the model for the loves of all the other Alexandrians. It is a lack of centrality like hers which is central to their seeking, and what they seek is the contriving of an integument whose surface is sensitive to the stimuli of the real outer world. When they succeed—which they often do for a brief time—their involvement along the entire periphery occupies all of their attention and keeps them from noticing that none of the sensation is reaching the interior where, in any case, there is nothing that can meaningfully engage it. Beneath the sensitized skin the whole Alexandrian museum turns out to be a display of specimens of psychic taxidermy.

This is strikingly developed by Durrell's use of the symbolism of masks and mirrors. Not only are faces masked but whole bodies are concealed by shapeless dominoes. This makes possible such melodramatic events as the murder of Toto de Brunel and the love affair of Amaril and the virtuous Semira. But more fundamentally, the coverings serve to conceal as well as to reveal the essence of the individual as he conceives or wishes it. They are, in fact, the chief means by which any part of the truth of a character can be expressed and communicated, for they afford the opportunity to take on an almost unlimited number of qualities which exist only in the wearer's fantasy or which come from outside and do not really belong to him.

Either way the purpose is served: a *gestalt* is assembled and attributed to the fantast, and this substitutes for a genuine personality. It is altogether fitting that the glimpses of these people which can be obtained in a mirror show only a flattened view from a single angle. Since the images have no depth, what the Alexandrians see there are facets, not faces. In a sense, the mirrors are masks, too, differing from the domino in that the fractional truths they convey are based on perceptions rather than concealments and therefore better suited to tell the viewer what the actor wants him to know. This is most especially true when one of the Alexandrians is looking at his own reflection.

The overt symbolism of masks and mirrors is accompanied by the conscious acting out of parts by the characters. Poor simple Darley is dismayed to discover, in Balthazar's *Interlinear*, how he has been cast in the role of decoy by Justine. His acting has been unwitting, but the others usually know what they are about. For Mountolive the role arises from his professional duties as a diplomat; the others have more private reasons. In essence they are seeking the inner truths about themselves, but this is not forthcoming because they too are hollow, and the only truth available to them is peripheral. There is no personal integrity or significance except as it may be inferred from the tangential contact, and the *Quartet* offers no novelistic proof that such an inference is valid. When Nessim tells Justine that he is weary of the eternal role-playing necessitated by his plot and says, "If only we did not have to keep on acting a part, Justine," she responds with, "Ah, Nessim! Then I should not know who I was."

By masking and mirroring the faces they put on to meet the faces that they meet, Justine and the other Alexandrian lovers are able to place before others, and keep before themselves, artificial constructions to stimulate and receive such love as they are capable of. That is, of course, the love of Narcissus for his reflection in the pool, and it shares with it the qualities of shallowness and of providing an idealized object for the affections, one which does not demand the giving up of total absorption in one's own fancied excellences. No attempt is made to look below the surface; there is nothing there, and anyway the surface is wholly satisfying—until somebody throws a pebble into the pool. The masks and the mirrors are symbols of the body itself as the beloved.

This being so, the investigation of modern love has led up the blind alley of narcissism. On this level, the *Quartet* has not kept its implied promise to show how salvation may be attained through love, since the love that it depicts is primitive, rudimentary, unrealized. The endless experimentation is neither free loving nor self-realizing but a compulsive search for the only true freedom, that which comes from voluntary commitment to another, not from acquisition but from identification. But Justine collects scalps, not hearts.

ii

The *Quartet*, we find, has not developed in the direction its composer intended, or at least announced. The theme of love has proved insufficient to his purpose, and each variation upon it has been left unresolved. Yet it is not a failure, for as we progress from one part to the next we are aware of another motif which has been present all along and which becomes the dominant one as the pattern unfolds. The permutations of love are now seen to be both preludes leading up to it and counterpoint accompanying and enhancing it as it emerges. This is the theme of the artist as seer, and its exemplar is Pursewarden. It is he who has the vision of the heraldic universe, the transcendental reality which is concealed from ordinary men as they struggle hopelessly toward it through the inadequate agency of their fragmented loves.

The first book of the *Quartet* presents the naive view of Justine's loves through the eyes of Darley. At its end he has retreated, baffled, to his island to ponder the mystery of Alexandria: "I had to come here in order to rebuild this city in my brain." To help him he has the three volumes of Justine's diary, the "folio which records Nessim's mad-

ness," and Balthazar's *Interlinear*. Most of all he has his
memories of "the time when for the four of us the known
world hardly existed," and the conviction that he must
find the meaning of what has happened to him and to all
of them as soon as he has succeeded in defining the "gravi-
tational field" of Alexandria and in reconstituting in his
imagination the ways in which it determined their inter-
locking lives.

In *Balthazar*, Darley's eyes are rudely and humiliatingly
opened to unperceived and hitherto unsuspected meanings, and he is ruefully forced to admit that even the
revelations in the *Interlinear* do not tell the whole story.
The point of the novel's structure begins to be made here:
a change of the vantage point from which the actions and
relationships are viewed changes our comprehension of
them, as it does Darley's. The dominant aspect of love in
this volume is deception and slipperiness. Love as we think
we know it is being wrenched out of the framework thus
far supplied by our assumptions which have been cleverly
reinforced by Durrell. Our equilibrium as observers is being disturbed.

In *Mountolive*, love is seen as subject to certain external
influences and pressures. The exercise of power comes to
the fore as motive, even replacing love. This occurs not
only in the professional life of Mountolive but also in
Leila's letters to him. Notable events, such as Pursewarden's suicide, are now seen to have had a political
significance—even a political motivation. In the final volume, however, a number of story threads which appeared
earlier are gathered together and woven into a new motif.
The theme of love by no means disappears—it is in fact
reinterpreted—but what looms largest before the reader
here is the vision of the artist. Pursewarden and his views
on art and reality are what count most in *Clea*. They easily
supersede the nominal subject of the entire *Quartet* and
speak most truly for Durrell himself.

The transition from the theme of love to that of art is facilitated by the fact that Justine's mode of loving is also the model for the self-love of the artist. It thus maintains the thematic unity of the *Quartet* and provides the basis for a new and crucial development, the escape from the blind alley of narcissism. The artist, especially as depicted in Pursewarden and Clea, succeeds through his art in apprehending reality directly. He is thereby enabled to transcend the emptiness of the self which is the chief affliction of the other Alexandrians.

Durrell has provided a graded progression of characters to show this, beginning with Arnauti, Justine's first husband. His novel, *Moeurs*, leaves out all mention of the loss of her child "for artistic reasons," and so fails to account for The Check, thus depriving his portrait of "Claudia" not only of consistency but of verisimilitude as well. Having proved unable either to depict Justine or to win her, he departs from our story a failure. By Durrell's definition, his art has not put him in touch with reality.

Next is Darley. Caught in the toils of the Alexandrian love-game, he is equally unconvincing as a lover or as an artist. He is passive, troubled, and insensitive. He can only reach vaguely for truth, but lacks the insight to know in which direction. The most that can be said for him is that when it is thrust at him he recognizes it while admitting that he could never have attained it himself.

Darley speaks of the days of Alexandria as "a tide of meaningless affairs . . . demanding of us nothing save the impossible—that we should be." Being depends upon comprehension, and Darley's is severely limited. Although he is able to see analytically that love as he experienced it could only be "a sort of skin language" keeping lovers bound to each other without permitting them to come very close together, his understanding never penetrates beyond the fact that for him loving is pain.

But even this degree of intellectual understanding is not

the same as artistic insight. Even when Darley attains a moment of illumination on first reading Pursewarden's letters to Liza, this does not enable him to write. The letters are a revelation to him:

> Literature, I say! But these were life itself, not a studied representation of it in a form—life itself. . . . Here illusion and reality were fused in one single blinding vision of a perfect incorruptible passion which hung over the writer's mind like a dark star—the star of death!

Pursewarden was saying to him from beyond the grave that only by being willing to lose one's life, to give up the narcissism which made one cling to it at all costs, could one attain the vision of a world within which art could truly function—and Darley read the words but missed the message. Capable of giving himself to Melissa, and even to Justine and Clea, he could not give himself to death and so could not penetrate the masks which life wore. He could experiment, search, and record, but he could not attain the direct apprehension of essence which was Pursewarden's triumph.

iii

Mutilation in the *Quartet* is often the symbol of the way to life, even in its ultimate form of the threat of death itself. Justine and Nessim feel this in their lovemaking at the moment when the Palestine arms plot is exposed and their lives are in danger: "How thrilling, how sexually thrilling, was the expectation of their death!" For some of the Alexandrians actual physical mutilation, whether congenital or acquired, leads to increased sensitivity and awareness, and so to reconciliation with living. Liza's blindness ultimately wins her Mountolive. Balthazar's loathsome disease rallies his friends and results in his rehabilitation. For others it goes awry when it is placed in the service of a false vocation. Leila's disfigurement by smallpox drives her into isolation; her attempt to control Mountolive's life and career by correspondence is a misuse of her power, and she loses him. Narouz's harelip, which facilitates his avoidance of society and his natural bent toward primitivism, leads him to cultivate his mystical powers. When he tries to use them to turn the political plot into a holy war he meets death by violence. Even the magnificent Scobie (one of the best comic characters in modern fiction) loses his life through his inability to control his transvestite "Tendencies." But of greatest importance in the *Quartet* is what mutilation does to the imagination of the artist.

Love is pain, and Pursewarden has experienced it to the full in his love for Liza. He feels it also for all reality. Clea says of him that he is "a man tortured beyond endurance by the lack of tenderness in the world." It is, of course, precisely this which enables him to set aside enough of his own narcissism to see the whole image in the cracked mirror and the true face behind the mask. But whereas the pain that is a concomitant of love is not enough to give more than a momentary glimpse of truth, the pain that drives the artist out of his narcissism enables him to master his medium by eliminating the hindering self. He can then see the truth by means of his art, and this is the only way open to men, says Durrell. In his view, it is impossible to attain it through loving alone, although loving is all that is available to those who are not artists. For artists a better way offers itself, beyond love, beyond self-love, more valuable and more lasting. This is Pursewarden's way.

He has felt the pain of love, and this has brought home its futility to him: "At first we seek to supplement the emptiness of our individuality through love, and for a brief moment enjoy the illusion of completeness. But it is only an illusion." Instead of joining the lovers to each other and the world, it actually separates them by making each aware of his own hollowness and of the world's unreality. Love having failed, it then becomes necessary to seek another road to fulfillment.

Pursewarden has discovered that art can perform an essential service for him. As he remarks to Balthazar, "The object of writing is to grow a personality which in the end enables man to transcend art." Art is not the end of the search but rather the chief portal through which one must pass in the quest. To emphasize this, Pursewarden tells Clea,

> Now in my life I am somewhat irresolute and shabby, but in my art I am free to be what I most desire to seem — someone who might bring resolution and harmony into the dying lives around me. In my art, indeed, through my art, I want really to achieve myself, shedding the work, which is of *no importance*, as a snake sheds his skin.

The object of art, then, is the discovery—or even the creation—of the self, the essential residue which is left when the dross of self-love is burned away. For the artist, the excessive self-love can be neutralized or destroyed, although Pursewarden finds this most difficult:

> I realized that to become an artist one must shed the whole complex of egotisms which led to the choice of self-expression as the only means of growth! This because it is impossible I call the Whole Joke!

In spite of his disclaimer, it is evident that he has done exactly that and has even shed the work itself. What is left is true; the artist now knows himself.

And he wishes to devote his hard-won knowledge to benefit the world. In the libidinousness and licentiousness of the story, the ethical intent of the *Quartet* is often overlooked, but it is quite plainly stated in the notebooks containing the discourses to Brother Ass where Darley reads what the world might be if only other artists could achieve and hold Pursewarden's vision and teach it to their fellow men.

I am full of hope. For always, at every moment of time, there is a chance that the artist will stumble upon what I can only call The Great Inkling! Whenever this happens he is at once free to enjoy his fecundating role; but it can never really happen as fully and completely as it deserves until the miracle comes about—the miracle of Pursewarden's Ideal Commonwealth! . . . only then shall we be able to dispense with hierarchy as a social form. The new society will be born around the small strict white temple of the infant Joy! . . . The great schools of love will arise, and sensual and intellectual knowledge will draw their impetus from each other. . . . Here art will find its true form and place, and the artist can play like a fountain without contention, without even trying! For I see art more and more clearly as a sort of manuring of the psyche. It has no intention, that is to say no *theology*. . . . Art is the purifying factor.

For Pursewarden, then, the artist is not simply the man who finds himself through art. He is rather one who has lost himself and found the world, the true world stripped of the self-deluding accretions which keep us from the enjoyment of primal innocence. He sees through the masks and past the mirrors, and his vision can open the eyes of others, enabling them to penetrate the incidental fragments which obstruct their line of sight on every side. The final step in the realization of the self, then, is that of the artist as seer, as prophet, as spiritual teacher who will enable mankind to break the trammels which inhibit the attainment of natural joy, the joy we were born with and which is our right. Pursewarden has produced a vision of a world without evil, a secular heaven with no hell.

iv

In the final volume of the *Quartet*, the three-dimensional presentation having been completed, Durrell proceeds to the roundingout of his thesis. Following the death of Pursewarden he drapes the mantle of the artist on Clea who, since she is contrast and complement to both

Justine and Pursewarden, unites the two themes of love and art. The *Quartet* began with the empty would-be lover and continued with the partly successful but ultimately frustrated artist. It concludes with Clea, talented, deep, and with the true artist's power to transcend the limitations of this world and enter into Pursewarden's heraldic universe. Durrell follows his announced intention of leaving an open-end pattern, but he does so only as regards the lesser, nonartistic characters; for his artists he relies on the standard device of the framework and brings the main action to a close.

Our earliest glimpse of Clea, while the others were caught up in the masking and acting-out of carnival, showed her alone in her studio, devoting herself to drawing. She has been disturbed by the consciousness that the hands in her portrait of Justine are not right and she spends the evening sketching them again and again. This occurs more than a year after the end of her relationship with Justine and signifies her emancipation from the futile Alexandrian love-game.

As Balthazar tells us, she had been at work on the portrait while Justine told of the loss of her child.

> The black gloves she wore in the portrait left a small open space when they were buttoned up—the shape of a heart. . . . Clea took and kissed the heart in the black glove. She was really kissing the child, the mother. Out of this terrible sympathy her innocence projected the consuming shape of a sterile love.

The inevitable outcome was that the affair ended when the portrait was finished. But she had never gotten the hands quite right, and it was in struggling with this problem that she occupied herself while Alexandria reveled. Freed from her bond to Justine, she still needed to come to terms with her womanliness and her artistry, and the fates of these two were inseparable.

Recognizing that what prevented her from working

effectively was her virginity, she took the startling but logical way of bursting in upon Pursewarden and desperately asking him to deflower her. With his usual tact he made exactly the right response: he laughed at her and, of course, refused. But he rendered her the valuable service of discussing her problem seriously and telling her that she was right. To create she would have to get her self out of the way. He told her,

> I believe that artists are composed of vanity, indolence, and self-regard. Work-blocks are caused by the swelling-up of the ego on one or all of these fronts. You get a bit scared about the imaginary importance of what you are doing. Mirror worship! My solution would be to slap a poultice on the inflamed parts—tell your ego to go to hell and not make a misery out of what should be essentially *fun, joy*.

The "treatment" was completed by Clea herself. Some months later, in Syria, she carried on a brief but genuine affair with Amaril in which Pursewarden's symbolic deflowering of her became actual. As the end of the affair approached—she knew Amaril was about to return to Alexandria and marry Semira—she found herself pregnant. It was at this point that she took the crucial step of having an abortion. Painful though the decision was, she recognized its necessity. The episode must be terminated; no burden from the past must be allowed to contaminate the coming marriage. For herself the meaning was especially profound: "It is funny but I realized that precisely what wounded me most as a woman nourished me most as an artist." Pursewarden's lesson had been well learned.

The twin themes of the sloughing-off of the self and the pouring of the released energies into art continue throughout Clea's story. She becomes Balthazar's clinic painter, recording lesions and anomalies for him. "The purely utilitarian object [of these pictures frees her] from any compulsion toward self-expression." But what is equally important about them is that their subjects are disease and mutilation. In Durrell's view, what makes Clea an artist is her suffering of a wound which frees her to create. She is also influenced by the factor of restitution. Having undergone deflowering and abortion, she uses her art to aid in healing. This is most strikingly illustrated in the episode of Semira's nose, constructed by the plastic surgery of Amaril after a design by Clea. Thus the wound-and-bow theory of creation is fully exemplified in the *Quartet*, culminating in the spectacular accident which results in the loss of Clea's hand and in her subsequent discovery about her prosthesis that "*It* can paint."

The sequence has been carefully worked out by Durrell, and his intention is unmistakable. First is the clumsy Darley who lacks both vision and ability and suffers because he has an uncontrollable itch to write. Next comes Pursewarden, seer, artist, and teacher, whose art enables him to avoid defeat by life until at last his commitment becomes too burdensome. Finally we are shown Clea whose progressive mutilations of body and spirit raise her above mundane necessities into the world of art, which is the world of reality undistorted by the distractions of living. It is this life beyond love and beyond art which is celebrated in the *Alexandria Quartet*.

THE ELEMENTS OF WILLIAM GOLDING

Irving Malin

WILLIAM GOLDING refuses to deal with conventional themes, characters, or situations. He avoids neat categories. He irritates us so much that we are tempted to label and forget him. Some critics have already done this (with great respect). Frederick R. Karl writes that Golding's "eccentric themes, unfortunately, rarely convey the sense of balance and ripeness that indicate literary maturity. . . ." James Gindin objects to his self-defeating "gimmicks." V. S. Pritchett calls his last two novels, *Free Fall* and *The Spire*, "obscure, strained, and monotonous." But Golding remains a problem.

Perhaps we can respond freshly to his works—are they novels or fables?—only if we question our usual critical assumptions. Do novels have to deal with social issues? What is artistic maturity? Is language as powerful as gesture? Such radical questions are avoided by the three critics mentioned above, who accept vague definitions of novelistic "reality." Golding asks himself these very questions—in his novels. He presents the constant battle between primitive levels of response and deceptive consciousness, the beast and the human. Because he tends to view this conflict within one being, he does not portray complex social character. His heroes are more aware of elemental nature than of social adaptation. They are flat and stylized; they do not seem to belong in novels (at least the ones we are used to).

Golding's psychology shapes his novels. He wants to give us the "poetry of disorder" (Richard Chase's phrase), not the science of order. But the very words he uses are logical; they discipline elemental nature, destroying some of its violent, sudden beauty. How can he express his *vision* of our primitivism when this very expression mutilates it? Golding's strange novels are, by their very nature, suicidal because they cannot capture those ambiguous gestures which are below (or above?) language. To claim that he does not know what he is doing; to assert that he is unnecessarily eccentric—such statements assume the incompetence of Golding, whereas they confirm the limitations of his critics.

But are Golding's views so unusual? If we look at Gaston Bachelard's criticism, for example, we see that he also recognizes the need for elemental return. He believes that science—any logical pattern—cannot comprehend reality: it is seduced often unwittingly, by what is "out there"; it disregards the elemental nature of life. "Fire is no longer a reality for science" because it—like earth, air, or water—becomes a simple datum of experience, not a complex object of reverie. Poetry, on the other hand, refuses to settle for deceptive measurement: it does not assume that "out there" can be separated from "in here"; it constructs an intuitive *field* of subject and object, reverie and element. *Golding's novels question and construct this same field.*

Lord of the Flies (1954) has been frequently discussed in the last few years in terms of Original Sin, the Freudian Trinity, and the Parody of *Coral Island*. But as Bern Oldsey and Stanley Weintraub have pointed out, it refuses to be conveniently categorized. They believe that the four boys—Simon, Piggy, Ralph, and Jack—are "endlessly" suggestive. Perhaps their most significant statement (for our purpose) is the following:

the major characters . . . are usually identified in the book with certain imagery and talismanic objects: Jack with blood and dung, with the mask of primitive tribalism (imagistically he is in league with the Lord of the Flies); Piggy with pig's meat (his physical sloth and appetite and eventual sacrifice), with his glasses that represent intellect and science (though they could hardly coax the sun into making fire); Ralph with the conch and the signal fire, with comeliness and the call to duty, with communal hope. (*College English*, November, 1963)

Lord of the Flies is more than an adventure story or allegory because of this very insistence upon "odd" objects. By placing his boys upon a mysterious island—where is it?—Golding forces them to explore the landscape. Earth, air, fire, water—these shape and hold the meanings of existence.

The four elements—the four boys. How convenient it would be if Golding were to equate them! Piggy and fire? Jack and earth? Simon and air? Ralph and water? But we feel cheated. There is no *one* element for each boy because Golding realizes that even "primitive life" remains mysterious. There is no doubt, however, that just as the Elizabethans employed the four humours—based on the four elements—he associates personality and element. This association is more lasting than the incantation of old names. The four boys constantly touch the elements, whether or not they realize they do. Because they are bound to different elements (in different combinations) they battle one another. And they torment themselves in their desire to rule (or be ruled by) only one element.

Throughout the novel Golding refers to the illusive quality of the island. Simon, for example, sees "a pearly stillness, so that what was real seemed illusive and without definition." Piggy peers "anxiously into the luminous veil that hung between him and the world." Jack peers "into what to him was almost complete darkness" when he first arrives on the beach. Because the elements are shadowy and ambiguous (and threatening?), they defy the vision of all the boys, including Simon and Piggy. Thus we have a completely ironic situation. The boys are forced to return to the elements—to exist "originally"—but they are so deceived by magical qualities that they cannot clearly judge their experience. Although many critics have complained about the gimmick at the end of the novel—the boys are saved; the officer doesn't "understand" the violence which has occurred—it is justified because it is another "appearance." The officer allows his "eyes to rest on the trim cruiser in the distance," but we doubt that he can see it or the water with full knowledge.

Lord of the Flies is therefore a novel of faulty vision. Can the boys ever see the elements? Are the elements really there? Is a marriage between elements and consciousness possible? The novel is not about Evil, Innocence, or Free Will; it goes beyond (or under) these abstractions by questioning the very ability to formulate them.

Look at any crucial scene. There is an abundance of descriptive details—the elements are "exaggerated" because they are all that the boys possess—but these details are blurred in one way or another. The result is, paradoxically, a confusing clarity. (Even the "solid" words the boys use are illusive: Piggy says "ass-mar" for asthma; Sam and Eric call themselves one name, "Sam 'n Eric.") Here is the first vision of the dead man in the tree:

> In front of them, only three or four yards away, was a rock-like hump where no rock should be. Ralph could hear a tiny chattering noise coming from somewhere—perhaps from his own mouth. He bound himself together with his will, fused his fear and loathing into a hatred, and stood up. He took two leaden steps forward.
> Behind them the sliver of moon had drawn clear of the horizon. Before them, something like a great ape was sitting asleep with its head between its knees. Then the wind roared in the forest, there was confusion in the darkness and the creature lifted its head, holding towards them the ruin of a face.

Golding gives us the short distance, the hulking object. Ralph (and the others) should be able to *see*. But he cannot. Although he "binds" himself—becoming more stable—he does not know where the noise comes from or what the "no-rock" is. His senses cannot rule the elements. He, like the lifted face, is a ruin.

V. S. Pritchett claims that *Lord of the Flies* indicates "Golding's desire to catch the sensation of things coming into us." On the contrary, it indicates his need to tell us that "out there" and "in here" never marry—not even on an enchanted island. We should not forget that the Lord of the Flies may be only a skull—an object given miraculous life because of faulty vision.

The Inheritors (1955) contains the same themes. Like the four boys, the "people"—Nil, Mal, Lok, Fa, and the old man—are fascinated by the elements, trying to understand them. Because they have never been exposed to the science of order—they are not British!—they are *closer* to fire, earth, air, and water than even Jack Merridew. They worship these; they are grateful to Oa. The elements are ritualized, not manipulated. When the old woman "wakes' fire—the fire is animate—she follows a definite but natural pattern: "She went quickly to the piles and came again with twigs and leaves and a log that was fallen almost to powder. She arranged this over the opened clay and breathed till a trickle of smoke appeared and a single spark shot into the air." Note the word "breathed." It signifies the communion between object and subject, the field of elemental existence.

Not only do these people marry the elements—they marry one another. They think in pictures: "Then, as so often happened with the people, there were feelings between them. Fa and Nil shared a picture of Ha thinking." These poetic and extralogical pictures are built around the elements. They do not seem faulty—like the visions in the previous novel.

Yet they are. These people cannot survive the arrival of human beings (semi-savages) who have invented canoes, combs, bows and arrows. They cannot cope with such ingenious logic; they cannot believe that the field between object and subject is broken. How can these newcomers *dominate* the elements? Why do they not worship Oa?

Golding places *us* in an *extraordinary situation* — as he always does to his characters. He knows that we want to sympathize with Lok and Fa, especially when their child is taken away, but we are so tied to science that we cannot. We are ambivalent. We stand between primitive responses and enlightened consciousness. We are the baffled inheritors of the battle in the novel. Golding's technique turns the screw. For eleven chapters he places us in the "no-minds" of the primitives. We see with their eyes (and limbs); we are married to them, even though we know more than they do. We accept the breath of new life. (The island itself is alive; it is a "seated giant.") But as we see more of the newcomers, we lose this elemental no-identity. We recognize ourselves in the inventors. In the last chapter (and slightly before it) Golding shifts the point of view — indeed, he establishes a logical pattern. We are "converted"; we are civilized. *And we feel lost.* Like Tuami we peer "forward past the sail to see what lay at the other end of the lake. . . ." But we now share his faulty human vision: we cannot see beyond the "line of darkness."

Some critics dislike *The Inheritors* because they cannot "deplore the loss of [Lok's] kind of innocence" (Walter Sullivan) or they find little to engage them (Frederick R. Karl). Perhaps they fight elemental return, afraid to surrender themselves to no-identity, if only for a short time. They hold fast to logic. By doing so they miss the real power of the novel — that power created by tension between innocence and knowledge, gesture and language. This tension is, unfortunately, all-too-human.

Pincher Martin (1956), like the previous novels, transports us to some place removed from the "old world." Here it is "a single point of rock, peak of a mountain range, one tooth set in the ancient jaw of a sunken world, projecting through the inconceivable vastness of the whole ocean—and how many miles from dry land?" We must explore it as does Pincher. It is ironic that the solid elements assume various shapes—that they are enchanted: "He stopped talking and lay back until the unevenness of the Dwarf as a chairback made him lean forward again." Because Pincher cannot leave his own mind, he cannot rule this brave new world.

Although he is the only human being in the novel, he creates conflict. He wants to dominate the elements (as do Tuami or the school boys); he cannot join them. We admire his strength of will, but we realize that he has broken the field between object and consciousness. He has violated some taboo. Pincher wants to devour the universe, to gorge himself with elemental food (and be reborn as some deity?) His body and mind are hungry. They eat each other. Throughout the novel Golding uses images of teeth, maggots, and lobsters: "The whole business of eating was peculiarly significant. They made a ritual of it on every level, the Fascists as a punishment, the religious as a rite, the cannibal either as a ritual or as medicine or as a superbly direct declaration of conquest. Killed and eaten." Unlike Lok and his group, Pincher cannot marry the elements, or perceive that mind, body, and essentials are the same "stuff." He starves.

Who is *he?* Do we know him well? What do we mean by character? By stripping Pincher of his civilized garments—only on page 76 do we learn his name—Golding dehumanizes him (according to our usual definitions of "human"). *He becomes it*—another element. The transformation is unpleasant because it is so radical. But only after we see this thing closely, do we realize that it was always less than human. Again Golding makes us ambiva-

lent. We fear this grasping thing—is it us too?—and admire its desire to survive. But he is less successful when he
introduces Pincher as a former actor, potential murderer,
and adulterer. We are startled. We lose our ambivalence.
We are so accustomed to the elemental Pincher that we
cannot accept his previous life as "real."

The underlying problem is that Golding is more interested in space than in time. Fire, earth, air, and water are
described powerfully. Golding plays with our infantile
fantasies—when we are engulfed by water or we fall suddenly: "He hutched his body towards the place where air
had been but now it was gone and there was nothing but
black, choking water. His body let loose its panic and his
mouth strained open till the hinges of his jaw hurt. Water
thrust in, down, without mercy." Space eats us. (Of
course, we could interpret such fears in a sexual way, but
again we are not deep enough. Golding is beyond the
problem of sex; sex is made up of the elements.) Time is
on a higher, rational level. It inspires complex terror; it is
more civilized (and civilizing). Golding's flashbacks appear artificial and convenient. Only when Pincher remembers in terms of drowning or claustrophobia—that is, *spa-
tially*—does he become interesting: "I'd lie in the hot,
rumpled bed, hot burning hot, trying to shut myself away
and know that there were three eternities before the dawn.
Everything was the night world . . . , the world of . . .
things harmless in the daytime coming to life, the ward-
robe, the picture in the book, the story, coffins, corpses,
vampires, and always squeezing, tormenting darkness,
smoke thick." This other world is "eternal" (as is the
world of Lok). Eternal space, although not particularly
pleasant, shapes horrifying beauty.

Golding's powerful description of this other world
creates problems. Words are not fire or water; they cannot
frighten us. We expect them to *describe* fear, not to
incarnate it. After fifty pages of even the most vivid poetry

of disorder, we become restless. We want more than elements. But Golding does not compromise (except for his flashbacks). He fights us, trying to drown us in these very elements. In a strange, otherworldly way, he has situated us as he has Pincher. The battle continues "eternally."

Free Fall (1959) deals primarily with time. Sammy Mountjoy tries to discover at what stage he fell from grace: "When did I lose my freedom? For once, I was free. I had power to choose." Of course, he is more social than any of Golding's previous heroes, but he shares their primitive qualities. He is placed in time—as they are cast *somewhere*. He must confront it with the same care they need to understand rocks or fire. Sammy's problem (as a human being and fictional character) is that he becomes obsessively involved with time, not knowing how to cope with it. It pinches his personality.

Frank Kermode has suggested that *Free Fall* is a "commentary." He is correct. Because Sammy likes to hear himself talk—if only to kill time—he indulges himself throughout the novel. He preaches; he gossips; he socializes. His commentary is his shield against elemental experience. It helps him to survive. But it also identifies him as a fallen creature who cannot commune with the elements. Only when Sammy discontinues his sermon—and this is relatively "impossible" in the novel—can he heal himself and become eloquent.

Several visions seem to escape from him. They are gestures of fear, grief, and wonder. They cannot be controlled (or distorted) by words, although they are expressed awkwardly by Sammy. Here is one:

> I was standing up, pressed back against the wall, trying not to breathe. I got there in the one movement my body made. My body had many hairs on legs and belly and chest and head, and each had its own life; each inherited a hundred thousand years of loathing and fear for things that scuttle or slide or crawl. I gasped a breath and then listened through all the working machinery of my body for

the hiss or rattle, for the slow, scaly sound of a slither, except that in the zoo they made no sound but oozed like oil. In the desert they would vanish with hardly a furrow and a trickle of sand. They could move towards me, finding me by the warmth of my body, the sound of the blood in my neck. Theirs was the wisdom and if one of them had been left at the center there was no telling where it would be next.

The images surround him; they assume a life of their own—like crawling things. They are "beyond" words—even his body and mind only "hiss" as they wait. His entire vision is eternal, presenting the "hundred thousand years of loathing and fear for things."

Thus *Free Fall* is a broken novel. Most of the time we have a rational (if—flowery) discourse. Sammy expounds at length. Only when he permits his visions to intrude—destroying the pretense of any philosophical conversation—does he lose himself and become interesting. The paradox is great. He is "wise" when his body—in touch with the many crawling things—speaks. This is his free fall.

Perhaps Golding's problem here can be stated in another way. He is unsure whether or not to be social. He refuses to accept Sammy's artificial talk for what it really is: *the mask of civilization.* (Remember Pincher as "actor.") He pushes down infantile fantasies. But these eventually rise to the surface and drown words. It is when Golding himself loses his ambivalence and submits to primitive gesture—or hallucination?—that his muse sings her best song of survival.

The Spire (1964) seems, at first, to be completely different from the earlier novels. It is set in the Middle Ages; it deals with a community of "civilized" people. But if we look more closely, we recognize Golding's usual themes (or obsessions?). Jocelin, the Dean, wants to impose his will—is it the Lord's?—upon the elements. He cannot allow the "air" to be free, he must build a spire to pierce it.

He forces others to fulfill this design. Is it *spiritual?* Is it *foolish?* Such questions are not answered rationally. But it seems likely that Golding is playing seriously with one real paradox: any religious pattern—no matter how much it tries to catch God—destroys the elements (at the same time it needs and uses them). By constructing the spire, Jocelin ruins the foundations of his own being. We are not really told about these. Golding implies, however, that the spire and the church itself resemble the male body: "The model was like a man lying on his back. The nave was his legs placed together, the transepts on either side were his arms outspread. The choir was his body; and the Lady Chapel, where now the services would be held, was his head. And now also, springing, projecting, bursting, erupting from the heart of the building, there was its crown and majesty, the new spire." The spire is erected by Jocelin as an act of love, but he forgets that it is physical *and* spiritual. In doing so he unwittingly kills his elemental totality—himself.

The novel gives us the vision of folly (as do all the others). Because Jocelin cannot see his own body-needs for worship, he gazes everywhere else. He stands high; he is dizzy. Not only are these repeated images of height realistic—they symbolize the spiritual adventures of Jocelin. He goes up, but he must fall; he must see his own *earth* as well as divine *air.* When Jocelin perceives his human limitations, he crawls with his face close to the ground: "So he crawled across the boards on hands and knees and the figure crawled towards him. He knelt and peered in at the wild halo of hair, the skinny arms and legs that stuck out of a girt and dirty robe. He peered in closer and closer until his breath dimmed his own image and he had to smear it off." This figure—also masked like Pincher?—is the Dean himself. The dirt cannot be smeared off, especially by flying away. Through his use of the elements, Golding reminds us that vision hugs the ground.

The Spire also contains silence. Although Jocelin is assaulted by the noise of rowdy fun, of cursing, and of prayer, he hears completely while he is "dumb." He admires the mute artisan who carves stone and hums:

> Then silence, both looking at the stone.
> Rushing on with the angels, the infinite speed that is stillness, hair blown, torn back, straightened with the wind of the spirit, mouth open, not for uttering rainwater, but hosannas and hallelujahs.

Silence is the "wind of the spirit"; it is free air. Jocelin cannot understand the words of the others who comfort him while he lies on his death-bed. He has no more use for earth-bound syllables. He longs for gesture. The novel ends with the visionary incarnation of sound into silence, element into spirit: "Father Adam, leaning down, could hear nothing. But he saw tremor of the lips that might be interpreted as a cry of: *God! God! God!* So of the charity to which he had access, he laid the Host on the dead man's tongue."

The novels of William Golding are successful—especially *The Spire* and *The Inheritors*—when they recreate the elements so well that we fall into silence.

DORIS LESSING:
THE FREE WOMAN'S COMMITMENT

Paul Schlueter

FEW POSTWAR British writers have had as prolific and successful a career or have so impressively presented support for a particular commitment to life and art as Doris Lessing. Since her arrival in England in 1949, she has produced an amazing and uniformly well-written and important array of books in almost every genre: six novels (including a series in progress called "Children of Violence"), five collections of short stories and novels, two volumes of autobiographical reminiscence and essays, as well as a slim book of poems and two successfully-produced plays. Born in Persia in 1919 and from her sixth year a resident of Southern Rhodesia (where, starting at the age of eighteen, she wrote and destroyed six novels), Mrs. Lessing in the years prior to her coming to England was once a Communist and twice a wife, to Frank Charles Wisdom, from 1939 to 1943 (by whom she has a son and a daughter), and Gottfried Anton Lessing from 1945 to 1949 (by whom she has a son).

Mrs. Lessing has been concerned in virtually all her fiction with problems which even this brief statement about her life and background suggests: the white-black struggles in southern colonial Africa, the physical and emotional relationships between men and women, the acute struggle of the "free woman" to survive and create for herself a meaningful life in a man's world, the left-wing

movements to which idealistic young people pledged their
allegiances in the 1930's and 1940's, and, especially in what
is surely one of the finest English novels of our time and
Mrs. Lessing's finest accomplishment, *The Golden Notebook* (1962), the role of the novelist in today's society.
Mrs. Lessing is frequently linked with two other woman
writers also concerned with sex, communism, and the "free
woman," but Mary McCarthy is considerably more acidly
satiric and self-consciously intellectual, and Simone de
Beauvoir is more deliberately "philosophical" and less a
novelist and craftsman than a propagandist. But the
unique thematic and conceptual qualities of Mrs. Lessing's
fiction, and the manner in which these are developed and
expanded, warrant a discussion of her as a major writer in
her own right, not merely as an English parallel to other
writers. For there is no one quite like, or even close to, Mrs.
Lessing in the intensity of her commitment both to the
social and personal issues suggested above and, also, to
certain theories of the novelist's craft.

In an extremely important critical statement, "The
Small Personal Voice" (published in 1958 in *Declaration*,
edited by Tom Maschler, in which Colin Wilson, John
Osborne, John Wain, Kenneth Tynan, and other younger
writers state their credos), Mrs. Lessing indicates that
commitment is necessary, partly because of today's confusion of standards and values, but also because of the compassion, warmth, humanity, and love of people to be found
in the truly great novels; because the writer has a responsibility as a human being to choose for evil or to strengthen
good; and, most important, because the writer's recognition of man as an individual is necessary if the novel as a
genre is to "regain greatness." To achieve greatness, she
states that the novelist's "small personal voice" must "recreate warmth and humanity and love of people," especially if a great age of literature is to result. Such a credo
does not, she says, necessarily become "propagandizing"

for a cause, political or otherwise; nor does the novelist necessarily regress by so committing himself. Rather, the novelist "must feel himself as an instrument of change for good or bad," as "an architect of the soul." As such an instrument of change herself Mrs. Lessing of necessity is concerned about the world of which she is and has been a part, most importantly Africa; and the relationships that do exist and should exist between whites and blacks in colonial Africa can be found in virtually all of Mrs. Lessing's books, from her first published novel, *The Grass Is Singing* (1949), to at least three of the five novels in the series "Children of Violence," to two collections of short stories, *This Was the Old Chief's Country* (1950) and *African Tales* (1964), to four of the five short novels in *Five* (1953), winner of the Somerset Maugham Award of the Society of Authors, 1954), and to a major part of *The Golden Notebook*.

The Grass Is Singing also introduced at least two types of characters frequently found elsewhere in Mrs. Lessing's fiction: the failure in one society or milieu who attempts to prove himself in another (in this book, Dick Turner), and the discontented woman who senses that life consists of more than the routine of daily life (Dick's wife, Mary). Mary, the novel's protagonist, and a former spinsterish urban office-worker, attempts to make a success of the farm she and her husband live on, and especially to treat the native workers in a stable, civilized fashion. Simultaneously attracted to and repelled by a native houseboy, Mary sadistically begins to abuse and punish the natives, regretting such treatment even while she gives it. The preferential treatment shown the whites by the law and the general callousness of the whites toward the Negroes becomes, by extension, a theme concerning Africa itself. As it concerns the Turners, it is culminated by the houseboy killing Mary in much the same way, as Frederick R. Karl has suggested Mario killed the magician in the

Thomas Mann novella. The whites, in short, become not
the masters but the slaves, as their commitment to a false
basis of civilization becomes the means of their destruction. A parable as well as a novel, *The Grass Is Singing*
makes its points about white responsibility toward black
Africa pointedly and disturbingly, and, to a lesser degree,
introduces another theme frequently found in Mrs. Lessing's later fiction, even in that not concerned with Africa,
namely, the ideal and real relationships between man and
woman. This parabolic quality is especially seen in the
sometimes forced manner in which the whites tenaciously
and foolishly cling together, even if personal animosity
exists between them, as if such identification makes their
relationship an island of white security in the midst of
black anarchy. For instance, when Dick's neighbor, considerably more successful than Dick, helps him despite their
obvious mutual dislike, we are told: "He was obeying the
dictate of the first law of white South Africa, which is:
'Thou shalt not let your fellow whites sink lower than a
certain point; because if you do, the nigger will see he is as
good as you are.'" Hence Mary's own conflict is all the
more intense and debilitating, as she senses her forbidden
attraction for the native and the conditioned hatred her
society forces upon her; and the ideal though unrealistic
and superficial social-worker attitude Mary at first holds,
which so easily becomes blatant and sadistic cruelty, illustrates the gulf, frequently seen in Mrs. Lessing's fiction,
between the hoped-for and the actual. Whether the issue
is racial, political, social, sexual, or personal, Mrs. Lessing's
characters frequently find themselves in conflict not only
with the world but with their own divided psyches.

As perceptive and disturbing as *The Grass Is Singing* is,
it seems in retrospect comparative apprenticeship work for
Mrs. Lessing's major work, particularly the five-novel series, "Children of Violence," three parts of which have
already been published (*Martha Quest*, 1952; *A Proper*

Marriage, 1954; and A *Ripple from the Storm,* 1958), with
the fourth due this year (*Land Locked*). Comparable in
scope and breadth with the series currently in progress by
such other contemporary British writers as C. P. Snow and
Anthony Powell, but surpassing these, I believe, in depth
of character analysis, this series tells of Martha Quest's
maturation and invitation into all the areas of life mentioned in the earlier works. Martha, a highly idealistic
young girl, desires not only to be "free" but also to change
the world in terms of criteria not shared by the white rulers
of colonial Africa. In her middle teens as the first book
opens, Martha avidly and widely reads about those subjects she finds of greatest concern (Havelock Ellis on sex,
numerous works on politics and economics), ultimately
discovering the conventional truth that such books have
little to do with sex and social institutions as they exist in
the real world.

Part of Martha's conflict is with her mother, who is
conventionally Victorian in both moral and racial attitudes. This conflict between generations, also to be found
to some extent in Mrs. Lessing's other books, takes on a
particularly poignant quality in the first novel of this series,
inasmuch as Martha's situation seems more than a little
based on the author's own early life. For instance,
Martha's "free" life, which seems so sacrilegious and im-
moral to her mother, leads her not only to question her
elders' beliefs but also to join a group of wildly iconoclastic
young men and women, whose lives seem to be exclusively
devoted to a carefree maintenance of their privileged way
of life, which she quickly discovers is shallow, selfish, im-
moral and unsatisfying. In the second volume of the series,
Martha, a few years older, decides to join the Communist
Party, early in World War II days. She leaves home, takes
a room in the city, experiences the feeling of being independent, deliberately encounters and even has affairs with
various types of people (such as Jews) toward whom domi-

nant opinion in her milieu would be prejudiced, makes
the inevitable mistakes, sexual and otherwise, in being
"free," and finds that the situation in Africa and in her life
is considerably more complex than she had realized. For
instance, a major part of Martha's social entanglements
concerns not white-black tensions but Afrikaans-English
antipathy; even though such tensions have always been
present in Martha's experience, only in her later teens does
she find out for herself the enormity and intensity of the
feelings involved in such a conflict. And as she enters her
twenties, now a young married woman, Martha finds that
being and remaining "free" requires of her not only a
rejection of the religious and social heritage of her family
and environment, but also the very social institutions she
had previously been so fond of, such as marriage and
motherhood.

In *A Proper Marriage,* Martha more formally and systematically breaks with tradition; in this volume, she is
consciously atheistic and officially communistic, she becomes openly and avidly an advocate of native independence and equality, and, by a series of events culminating in
leaving her husband and child, she discovers the "real"
Martha and finds out that life does have meaning. Constantly obsessed with self-analysis, Martha's entire life in
these first two books is a movement toward certain half-
realized but irresistible goals, such as gaining some sort of
"freedom"; so long as Martha questions and searches, it
seems, her life tenaciously goes on, particularly so when
her searching first begins in the earlier volume. Certain
events of a melodramatic nature one might have expected
—such as an affair with a native or a collapse into neurosis
—fortunately do not occur; but one is left with the feeling
at the end of volume two that disaster of some sort is immi-
nent. For Martha, never having felt that she was loved by
her mother and never quite loving others, attempts in the
communist cause to discover an outlet for her long-

suppressed idealism and frustrated altruism. The Party, of course, is not quite the utopian, selfless situation she had dreamed of and wished for; the petty, peevish squabblings experienced in this commitment do not differ materially from the endless misunderstandings she had experienced at home and in marriage.

The third volume in the series, A *Ripple from the Storm*, concerns Martha's devoted service to communism, her encounter with other like and unlike spirits in the Party, her second marriage, to a German refugee who is himself a Communist of far greater intensity of commitment than Martha's, and the marriage's ultimate breakup. This volume, the least satisfying of the three thus far issued (primarily because of its more obvious polemicizing and Martha's less personal involvement in the world in which she lives), presents Martha overshadowed by the social institutions of her time, whereas, in the earlier two volumes, she greatly overshadowed those institutions. The perpetual political bickering and detail (comparable for seemingly encyclopedic endlessness only with the seventy-odd pages devoted to Martha's physical and emotional reactions to pregnancy in A *Proper Marriage*) are concerned in particular with the changes in colonial Africa's rather simplistic white-black antagonisms, such as the effects on white African society of two classes of new residents, the Jewish refugees from Germany, and the Royal Air Force personnel so outspokenly and ubiquitously subversive of colonial mores. The really important question to be faced and solved by colonial Africa (the racial situation) becomes overshadowed by fears of Communist inroads and attempted takeovers of African society, and the resultant, inevitable reaction of the earlier white settlers. The disillusionment necessarily resulting from the Communists' inability to solve Africa's problems, and Martha's corresponding ennui, caused by both political and personal failure, is bound to be of paramount concern in the fourth volume in the series, at this writing still unpublished; and if Martha Quest in this forthcoming volume continues to parallel Mrs. Lessing's own circumstances, emigration to England can also be expected. Even though the freshness and vividly authentic qualities of African life in the first book of the series, which was dropped in favor of political and marital maneuverings in the second and third, are not likely to be revived, it is not too extravagant to expect that Martha's initial effervescence and hopefulness in such an emigration will parallel somewhat the enthusiasm and idealism of her early teens. For it is certain that the commitment Mrs. Lessing is so concerned about in all her fiction will continue to be a part of Martha Quest's own life, even though the particular commitment may be somewhat altered from the youthful idealism or mature communism Martha Quest has already experienced.

The "Children of Violence" series was interrupted after the third volume for a novel which has come not only to be Mrs. Lessing's best known and most widely praised work, but also one of the most significant, original pieces of fiction written in the postwar years. Aside from the all-absorbing power with which Mrs. Lessing's familiar themes are developed, and aside from the magnificent writing with which the book abounds, it is important on purely structural grounds, since it, probably more than any single novel mentioned in this book, attempts to make the novel as a form do more than it has done in this generation, and to present, in an admittedly complex and complicated manner, the several identities of the human psyche, to develop these identities in parallel and contrapuntal fashion, and to carry the entire series of relationships these identities imply through both time and space. But it is considerably more than a virtuoso performance, more than a clever *tour de force* of incomprehensibility. Despite the novel's complexity of form, it contains perfectly comprehensible characters, incidents, relationships between people, and language; its complexity arises more from a structural than a stylistic technique.

Briefly stated, *The Golden Notebook* concerns Anna Wulf, an expatriate African, a former Communist, a divorcee, author of one successful book (she and her daughter live on the royalties), and an indefatigable keeper of four notebooks. In a black notebook, she keeps a chronological first-person account of her days in Africa; in a red, a first-person account of her days as a Communist; in a yellow, a fictionalized third-person account of a woman closely paralleling Anna herself; and in a blue, a diary of Anna's "present" activities and thoughts, encompassing all the other notebooks and, to some extent, paralleling their contents. The notebooks are divided into fourths, each fourth (in the sequence listed) presented as part of a major portion of the book, and each of these portions prefaced by a section entitled "Free Women."

The "Free Women" sections constitute a running third-person narrative (again in the "present" tense), which not only makes coherent sense read as an entity itself (since these sections are printed in a typeface different from that used for the rest of the book, this was evidently intentional), but which also parallels an attempt made by Anna toward the end of *The Golden Notebook* to "write" a tale beginning with the sentence which, in fact, begins the first "Free Women" section. In addition, there is another section of the novel as a whole also entitled "The Golden Notebook," which brings Anna's activities in the four major notebook sections to a kind of culmination; this section serves, more than anything else, to record the attempt to integrate the several Annas encountered in each of the earlier notebooks. But a love affair with an American writer, to which Anna clings, as described in this section, as a means of maintaining her sanity, collapses in a hopeless tangle of similarly tangled psychotic prose. Anna,

in this section, not only sees what each of the previous
Annas has been like, but also the mess that her life has
become, symbolized by her wild attempts to recapture the
irrevocably lost past through frantic pasting of newspaper
stories on her walls. A "Free Women" section concludes
the novel (again integrated with the earlier "Free
Women" sections) in which Anna, in a last desperate
struggle to find commitment and meaning in life, decides
to "join the Labour Party and teach a night-class twice a
week for delinquent kids." Anna's close friend, Molly
(who appears in all the "Free Women" episodes and, in a
thinly-disguised form, in the yellow notebook as well), also
a divorcee, commits herself to marriage; evidently both
women, having tried the other commitments possible in
such lives as theirs, cling even to such presumably-
exhausted remedies as marriage, politics, and social work,
so desperate in their search for meaningful and more permanent relationships.

In theme, *The Golden Notebook* parallels Mrs. Lessing's other novels, and in some ways develops the themes
to their logical extreme. Anna Wulf appears at times to be
a middle-aged Martha Quest, with the same history, the
same concerns and interests, the same all-encompassing
obsession with self-analysis, freedom as a woman in a
man's world, and the desire to commit oneself to some
lasting, satisfying *raison d'être*. Anna presumably is a representative "free woman," concerned not only with the self-
analysis with which contemporary novels abound, but also
with important issues of the larger world—political, social,
literary, racial, etc. Highly intelligent and sensitive to human desires and motivations, Anna chooses deliberately to
be what she is, and, with manifest self-dignity, creates her
own life. She never feels sorry for herself, nor does she
engage in the kind of nastiness sometimes found in the
heroines of the writers mentioned earlier as comparable to
Mrs. Lessing. Both Anna and Molly are indefatigably

strong, physically as well as mentally; they neither ask for nor give any quarter, either of men or of the world. In short, they (and especially Anna) have made a success of the life dreamt of by Martha Quest and others in Mrs. Lessing's fiction. So believable and powerful is Mrs. Lessing's character portrayal that it is safe to say that she has no peer in evoking the particular emotional states so obviously sought in this book. Probably more than in any other novel, *The Golden Notebook* captures the authentic quality of what it is to be a woman, especially a woman in a man's world, and even more especially a woman who frankly admits the existence of her sexuality, her neuroses, her intellect, her desperation in living, her disgust at the mediocre so feverishly sought by those of either sex who are themselves mediocre, her refusal to compromise her essential being. All of this makes what would be, in other hands, a mere experiment in bitchiness, a sensitive, perceptive, and manifestly universal account of great importance. Combined with the writing (certainly close to the best currently available on either side of the Atlantic) and the technical skill and accomplishment, the result is significant indeed. And despite the few critical disclaimers (such as the statement, "when a novelist writes a novel about a novelist writing about what we know the real novelist has written, we have a right to object"), *The Golden Notebook* stands as a fictional monument.

Several other books, of necessity to be treated briefly, have appeared since Mrs. Lessing first arrived in England. *This Was the Old Chief's Country* (1950), as already mentioned, is primarily concerned with black Africa. The theme in these stories is frequently the white man's insensitive assertion of his dominance over the natives and his feeling that the natives are amoral, irresponsible, and scarcely human. The book, in brief, is occasionally poignant and usually sensitive to the black Africans' situation, in ways unique among white African writers. *Five* (1953) makes this distinction between color groups even more vivid and important and is equally as sympathetic to the natives' feelings as the previously mentioned book. *Retreat to Innocence* (1956) is a novel about Julia Barr, who desires a more stable, uninvolved life different from that which her materialistic parents provide. In love with a Communist writer as old as her father, Julia senses her own lack of commitment and his impassioned dedication, and, since he cannot stay in England and she cannot dedicate herself to his cause and follow him, they separate. Although Julia has no "cause" to fill the void left by his leaving, it is clear that even communism is preferable to the sterility of a meaningless and undedicated existence. *The Habit of Loving*, a group of stories published in 1957, is set in various places—England, Africa, the Bavarian Alps—and is less concerned with political than psychological and sociological matters, such as in the long story, "The Eye of God in Paradise," which concerns the psychological reactions of two vacationing English doctors, a man and a woman, who find a mental hospital in postwar Germany more identifiable as naziism than as therapeutic medicine. *In Pursuit of the English*, a fictionalized series of reflective autobiographical sketches about England, appeared in 1960; it is concerned with the problems of becoming acclimated to a new country, and, among other matters, states Mrs. Lessing's conviction that her life "has been spent in pursuit," particularly of love and fame, which are both unattainable, and which fact took her a long time to discover. *Going Home* (1957), a series of inter-related but distinct essays, is concerned with Mrs. Lessing's return visit to Africa in the middle 1950's. In this book she makes explicit her feeling that overt political action and commitment is necessary, and—primarily because of the Hungarian situation then in the news—she provides a worthwhile, although somewhat ambivalent, discussion of the appeal of communism. *A Man and Two*

Women (1963), a collection of stories, emphasizes in particular the sensitivity of insight and intelligence in contemporary man and woman; less deeply felt or committed than in the other books, the characters in this volume are more like sketches or outlines of people than fully-developed people. "To Room 19," one of the best stories in this collection, is concerned with Susan Rawlings, whose well-run and rational world disintegrates; a partner in a marriage "grounded in intelligence," Susan finds isolation from her husband more and more a necessity, since their rational relationship lacks so much, and finally discovers death the only solution for her ennui. And *African Stories* (1964), as already mentioned, is concerned again with life in Africa with the natives' lives of paramount importance.

In addition to these books, Mrs. Lessing has published—and had successfully performed—two plays. The first, *Each His Own Wilderness* (1959; produced in 1958), concerns a liberal, committed, and, above all, free woman, Myra Bolton, who desires personal freedom, even to the extent of saying, "I don't propose to keep my life clutched in my hand like small change." The other play, *Play with a Tiger* (1962, produced in the same year with Siobhan McKenna in the lead), is a dramatization of the last scene in *The Golden Notebook*, in which Anna Freeman (Anna Wulf's maiden name) is involved with the American writer. As a play this scene seems more explicitly a war of the sexes, particularly a war unique with Anna's generation, in which disillusionment and such events as the Spanish Civil War were paramount, and which is contrasted with the present-day situation in which a younger generation finds itself aloof, unconcerned and uncommitted to any cause, and seemingly aware of only the faceless anonymity of existence in the world of the 1960's, with the threat of annihilation everpresent.

With such a phenomenally rich array of books in such a

short period of time, and with none of the books really a failure, one could expect that Mrs. Lessing's productive enthusiasm would be on the wane; instead, with (at this writing) two novels in the "Children of Violence" series yet to appear, and with the genius and imagination necessary to produce such a major work as *The Golden Notebook* not yet affected by signs of declining abilities (after all, Mrs. Lessing is only in her forties), one can legitimately expect a continued stream of profound, sensitive, and—above all—committed books in the future. For the commitment she has made to writing, the commitment she as a free woman has found most meaningful in our world today, is an opportune and gratifying one, and is likely to become one of the most felicitous commitments ever made to English literature.

IRIS MURDOCH:
EVERYBODY THROUGH THE LOOKING-GLASS

Leonard Kriegel

IRIS MURDOCH appears to be on the verge of achieving a major reputation in contemporary English fiction, and, as is so often the case today, hers is an achievement that does not depend upon any single work. It is rather the totality of her work which we are asked to examine, and it is that totality with which we are meant to be impressed. Miss Murdoch is prolific enough. Since 1952, she has published eight novels, her short and incisive volume on Sartre, and a number of philosophic and literary essays. One continues to expect a distinctly major work from her, and one is continually disappointed. Her very promise as a novelist can be compared to the promise of a novelist such as Norman Mailer, with whom she shares little else (except, perhaps, an essentially cataclysmic idea of sexuality). One expects great things from Mailer; one has expected them since the publication of *The Naked and the Dead* in 1947. And yet, for all their rage and anger, Mailer's novels are curiously lacking in reality, inescapably linked to the Portrait of the Artist as Aging Boxer that one finds inside the pages of *Esquire* rather than to any artistic reality they contain in themselves. Still, one continues to hope and to expect and even to sympathize because what there is remains so potentially good. Miss Murdoch's novels represent a weightier artistic performance than do Mailer's; she is neither sloppy nor blowzy nor guilty of that rhetorical shooting-from-the-hip which Mailer too frequently substitutes for craft. But she leaves us, as he does, essentially unsatisfied, expecting something more, some synthesis of myth and contemporaneity that will do what great art alone can do, fuse past and present and future in a vital crystallization of our world. And it is in just this, that quest for reality toward which the novelist must bend his efforts, that her novels seem curiously lacking. Her novels contain the language of ideas, but what they lack is the reality of flesh touching flesh (and this despite the great deal of sexual busyness in her books, almost all of it sex without salt and gesture without touch).

To her credit, Miss Murdoch has brought the free play of intelligence to the task of the novelist; she has taken the chances a novelist must take with language and she has emerged with a clear, incisive, determined prose; she possesses a sense of craft and an obvious dedication to the demands that novel writing make upon one; and she has accepted a world complex enough to make even the absence of tragedy endurable. She possesses humor and broad human sympathies, but for all of its turbulence and violence her world is surprisingly calm. What she lacks is rage (a quality which Mailer possesses in abundance), and her novels impress one as containing order at the expense of rage. The world she creates is permeated with too much Victorian insularity; it is not our world. Sartre, Miss Murdoch noted, "is profoundly and self-consciously contemporary; he has the style of the age." It is an accurate observation, and it leads one to the further observation that what is missing in Miss Murdoch's own work is that very "style of the age," that contemporaneity which she sees so clearly in Sartre. Interestingly enough, the novel of hers which is most clearly contemporary is her first, *Under the Net* (1954).

As a novel, *Under the Net* comes close to creating the fusion its author desires. The protagonist, Jake Donaghue, is not only interesting but also touching. He establishes a selfhood without having to force us into the world of symbolic counterplay. The first person prose—Jake is the narrator—is loose, buzzing with great nervousness, and human; we like Jake for his manner of telling as much as for what he tells. A seeker who wishes to make sense of the world, he is caught under the net of language. A lover who imposes an illusion of self as well as an illusion of others on his world, he has chosen as his "destiny" Hugo Belfounder, a former fireworks magnate and now a successful motion picture producer. For Jake, "we all live in the interstices of one another's lives, and we would all get a surprise if we could see everything." But Jake's reality is a Hugo who never has existed and who never will exist, just as Hugo's reality is a Jake wholly unlike the Jake we come to know. Nor is it Jake and Hugo alone who cannot truly see each other; the net is spread for all, since dependence upon language destroys the possibilities of true contact. Each character in the novel is illusory, at least insofar as he has to be verbalized by another in order to become a person. Hugo is the mythical father for whom Jake is searching (a search that Miss Murdoch turns into a skillful parody of all the search-for-the-father novels in western literature); Anna Quentin, who loves Hugo and is loved by Jake, is the mythical mother. Jake wanders through Paris and London looking for Hugo, only to find himself conspicuously unsuccessful until he finally takes a job as an orderly in a hospital. Hugo inevitably finds himself a patient in Jake's ward, and the two of them engage in a long nighttime conversation which ends with Jake's realization that Hugo is neither the lover nor the philsosopher of silence he had invested him with being; instead, Hugo is, like Jake himself, a man struggling to come to terms with his own reality. Hugo ends by giving his wealth to a socialist organization and leaving England so that he can become a watchmaker and make things with his hands. All of Jake's ideas about the interrelationships of people prove to be wrong; Hugo is not being cheated but is selling his film interests to Anglo-French Films; it is Sadie Quentin, not Anna, whom Hugo loves; and it is Jake whom he sees as a philosopher, not himself. Hugo will become a watchmaker, for to Hugo God is now "a task. God is detail. It [watchmaking] all lies close to your hand."

Jake, on the other hand, having finally been freed by Hugo of his own illusions about others, having finally been freed, in a sense, of the illusion of language, lends Hugo a half crown (the reversal of money roles is especially significant, since Hugo's wealth is a concomitant of Jake's illusion of him), and returns to his lodgings at Mrs. Tinckham's, prepared now to end his existence as a translator and to begin a new life as a writer. As the net of language is drawn tighter, it disintegrates; in so basic a paradox does Miss Murdoch conclude her first novel. The only sense, finally, that Jake can make of the world is the sense that art imposes on it. "It was the morning of the first day."

Under the Net is not the most impressive of Miss Murdoch's novels, but it is the one most filled with life. To see the world through Jake's eyes is to see a world that is both colorful and exciting. And the reality of his world is never in doubt. While it is not a very ambitious novel, it is a very good one. And while Miss Murdoch has come a long way since its publication, one wonders whether she does not need to recapture in her work the vitality that a narrator like Jake Donaghue gave to it. *Under the Net* is strong exactly where most of her later novels are weak, in its sense of life lived vitally.

In *The Flight From the Enchanter* (1956) the fusion of myth and politics, of psychoanalysis and religion, is given us in an occasionally brilliant but finally shallow novel. It fails because it is not rich enough. In a novel purporting to be another investigation of reality, Miss Murdoch uses characters as if she were peppering her artistic landscape with buckshot. There are so many characters bound together within this rather obtuse plot that the reader is virtually commanded to invest each one with some sort of symbolic significance. But significance cannot be symbolic alone. Mischa Fox, for instance, here has the Hugo Belfounder role; like Hugo, Mischa is an "enchanter," a being whose power is in large part what his lover-slaves demand of him. But where Hugo's appeal lies in his own very confused humanity, Mischa is so endowed with the aura of the allegorical that the reader simply cannot accept him. He is obtrusively comic because he is not really threatening; yet his role in the novel is as the center of imposed reality, and such a role cannot stand up to unintentional comedy. At one point, after Rosa Keepe hurls a paperweight at a bowl full of fish which breaks, Mischa leaves his own party and drives to the sea with Annette Cockeyne (another of Miss Murdoch's perpetual virgins). But the identification of Mischa with the sea, which Miss Murdoch wishes to achieve, is an identification imposed on us. It is not an organic part of the novel.

"The notion that one can liberate another soul from captivity is an illusion of the very young," says Calvin Blick, Mischa's woman-hating and somewhat sinister keeper of reality, to Annette. It is here that *The Flight From the Enchanter* is most philosophically effective; once again, Miss Murdoch depicts for us the breaking of illusion. Not that illusion is solely the property of the young; in Miss Murdoch's work, in fact, life seems most illusion-ridden not at twenty but at forty. And romantic illusion is the center of our sickness in all of her novels. Annette lacks what Calvin Blick has, the Calvinist view of life. Calvin, in turn, lacks compassion. And so we are blocked at all turns. For where illusion exists, one inflicts pain on oneself for its own sake; and where illusion does not exist, one inflicts pain on others.

From the very first page, however, the reader is seized by a sense of strain that seems impervious even to the acknowledged brilliance one finds in some of the novel's effects. The whole thing simply does not hang together very effectively. If Rosa Keepe is the center of consciousness in the novel, then what is one to make of her fascination with Mischa? Is it merely a repetition of the Jake-Hugo relationship? Is it a political allegory about the meeting of East and West? Or is it a statement about the necessity of myth for the modern world? A novelist has every right to purposeful ambiguity. And perhaps it is such ambiguity that Miss Murdoch is striving for. But her novel is finally much too playful, too intent on the effects of its own paradoxes (western Protestant liberalism saving its magazine, *The Artemis*, from Mischa Fox by rallying forces that are already really dead), too quick in seeking effects and too shallow in creating character to be truly successful. If we once again turn to Miss Murdoch's book on Sartre, we find another comment that is illuminating when applied to what she herself has written. The novelist, we learn, is "a sort of phenomenologist" whose eye is "fixed on what we do, and not on what we ought to do or must be presumed to do." But in *The Flight From the Enchanter*, with its Kafkaesque Polish brothers and its violated innocents, what we do becomes little more than a quest for the bizarre. If taken only as allegory, the novel might work; but it is not allegory; it is a rather somber satire and it fails, finally, because of its own weight. By the novel's end, Annette recovers from her attempted suicide because of her youth (that, at least, is not illusion) and Rose Keepe chooses Peter Saward, the scholar, over Mischa Fox, the enchanter. In each case, the choice is of the human over the supernatural. For us, both choices are healthy. But they come rather late to make much difference.

Miss Murdoch's third novel, *The Sandcastle* (1957) is her simplest. The novel is uncomplicated; its canvas is uncrowded; but although it deals, like *Under the Net* and *The Flight From the Enchanter*, with the destruction of romantic illusion, it is always distant—it lacks the warmth of *Under the Net* or the sharpness of *The Flight From the Enchanter*. (It unfortunately shares with *Flight* a kind of symbolic cuteness—witness the Tarot pack of cards and the figure of the mysterious gypsy who disappears when Rain Carter leaves.) *The Sandcastle* is a curious book. It is, for instance, the only one of her novels that contains a reference to left-wing politics, in which Miss Murdoch herself is interested. The protagonist, William Mor, is to stand as a Labour Party candidate for Parliament; he is also working on a book entitled *The Nature of Political Concepts*. But in a character so seemingly ineffectual, so completely abject and apologetic before his wife, all the reader is aware of in Mor's politics is the seeming incongruity and the oddly jarring note; Mor is simply too much what Miss Murdoch wants him to be, the submissive, browbeaten, somewhat servile husband. And what Mor is, the novel is. It lacks the strength it should have because its protagonist does not interest us as, say, the protagonist of Orwell's *Coming Up For Air* interests us. Miss Murdoch plays with her characters, moving them here and there in an effort to get things really underway. The relationship between Mor and Rain Carter, the young artist with whom he falls in love and who becomes the grail for his questing romanticism, is realistically and clearly done, but it is not at all moving. This may, of course, be Miss Murdoch's intention; romantic foolishness is her theme and there is no reason why she should sympathize with Mor. And she does see the family as a community in itself; the actions of Mor's wife, son and daughter are attempts to keep the community intact. Mor is finally lured from his romanticism by his wife, Nan; by his son, Donald, who sensationally climbs a tower to recapture the family's cohesiveness; by his daughter, Felicity, who attempts to bring Mor back to the fold through magic; by his colleague Bledyard, who, himself in love with Rain, wishes Mor to abdicate because Rain's painting has lost its realism; and by Tim Burke, who holds before him the promise of a political career. On the other side is Demoyte, Mor's elderly mentor, who urges him to run off with Rain and to succeed where Demoyte himself (he is a bachelor, apparently unloved and unloveable) and his kind have all failed; and, of course, Rain herself, with her rose garden loveliness and her green Riley sedan. But while Mor weighs the balance, Rain chooses for both of them. She leaves. And Mor remains with his parliamentary career before him, with his family intact, and with his illusions perhaps far more unshattered than the reader would like to believe.

Although Mor's story should be quite funny, Miss Murdoch chooses never to make him a figure of comedy. For whatever reason, he is treated with warmth and sympathy. Perhaps Miss Murdoch was too close to her sources when she wrote the novel, but she manages to confuse distance with detachment. And it is detachment she needed. What is good about *The Sandcastle* is its sanity and its use of the family as the center of civilization. What is bad about it, however, is its lack of intensity—the fact that the reader is so uninvolved in the affair between Mor and Rain Carter is a sufficient indictment on this count. And it comes as close to being boring as anything Miss Murdoch has written. We learn little from Mor's experience, and we wonder, finally, whether the experience itself was necessary.

The intensity lacking in *The Sandcastle* is abundantly present in *The Bell* (1958), Miss Murdoch's fourth and finest novel. For here we have a novel which, while it borders on the edge of Gothicism never steps over the line, a novel in which symbols are a part of the total effect rather than an excessively conscious manipulation of the writer's artistry. Few other novels published in English over the past twenty years have so successfully blended myth and reality.

For the most part, the action of *The Bell* takes place at Imber Court, a country estate which has been converted into a semi-official religious lay community attached to an Anglican nunnery. The members of the community have been drawn to Imber by their own illusions about religion (the one seeming exception to this is James Tayper Pace). What is lacking in the community is what is alive for the nuns in the abbey, whose vocation is the religious and who love God not under the delusion of selflessness but with the fulfillment of selfhood.

One of the rules at Imber Court is that one never discusses the past. It is this rule that Dora Greenfield is informed of soon after her arrival. But Dora's past life makes it difficult for her to accept the life at Imber Court; she cannot make of it the refuge from the real which the other members of the community seek within its grounds. It is significant that Dora, when told by her husband Paul about the nun in the fourteenth century who committed suicide by rushing into the lake and drowning herself because she had been called upon to confess her sins of the flesh, feels sympathy for the nun. It is also significant that the one other person to whom Paul relates the story, Catherine Frawley, tries to duplicate the nun's feat and is rescued from her medievalism only by Mother Clare, the abbess who possesses the capacity for life that is singularly lacking in most of the members of the lay community. Dora is the person within the lay community who is closest in spirit to Mother Clare. Catherine Frawley, on the other hand, had planned to enter the convent, but her plans are a manifestation of the romantic yearnings of a young girl in love with the homosexual lover of her own brother; Catherine distrusts life, as does her brother Nick, the

satanic element in the novel (a Satan who, like his ancestor, makes God a necessity). It is Dora's acceptance of life
which enables her to escape the ends destined for the
Frawleys (Catherine suffers a breakdown after her attempted suicide and Nick succeeds where his sister had
failed); Dora loves and is willing to be loved.

In the scene in which Nick exercises his power over
young Toby Bashe—to whom Michael has made
advances—he becomes an inverted Christ. Nick's message,
that "we are sinners one and all," embodies the Byronic
religiosity which leads one to an insistence on the devil's
reality if only for the purpose of petulantly screaming at
God the Father. And Catherine's attempted suicide is the
act of a little girl denied her wish; she loves Michael, as
little girls love those who are unaware of their love and
would be incapable of returning love even if they were
aware. In her little girl's way, she is involved with sin;
Dora, on the other hand, is involved with being. She is
closest to Mother Clare in her desire to live life rather than
to affirm death. (Making a nun the embodiment of the life
impulse, to the extent that she seems the most physically
alive character in the novel, is an excellent example of Miss
Murdoch's affinity for paradox.)

What the community of Imber Court suffers from is not
an excess of piety but an excess of illusion. And their chief
illusion is about Imber Court itself, for this retreat from
the world is corrupting, offering the illusion of innocence
in place of the true vocation enjoyed by Mother Clare.
The suffering that we find in *The Bell* is not merely
allegorical; it is real suffering, and the reader experiences
Nick's suicide as he experiences few other deaths in Miss
Murdoch's work. The bell itself symbolizes the failure of
Imber Court to relate to real suffering. On its rim is
written, "*Vox ego sum Amoris. Gabriel vocor.* 'I am the
voice of love. I am called Gabriel.' " But it is the choosing
of the illusion of sin over the reality that love offers which

accounts for the horror of Nick's suicide and Catherine's mental wreckage. It is the illusion of sin that prevents Michael from giving Nick the love he so desperately needs. "Nick had needed love and he, Michael, ought to have given him what he had to offer, without fears about its imperfection. If he had had more faith he would have done so, not calculating either Nick's faults or his own."

Like Michael, the devotees of Imber Court are, at least until the new bell falls into the lake, far too concerned with their imperfections to be able to love. Michael's failure is their failure. Afraid of his own homosexual yearnings, Michael loses sight of Nick's need. The rejection is, in large part, a rejection of self. And it is this which gives *The Bell* its ultimate power—Michael realizes what he has done; he is determined to make amends, to accept whatever responsibility he can for Catherine, although he cannot love her as he had loved her brother. It is a rather depressing end for Imber Court, an end only made somewhat more palatable by the fact that Dora survives. Her survival is gratefully accepted by the reader, for she will love again. It is her novel, not Nick's. We are all sinners, but we are also people who breathe.

Miss Murdoch's next three novels, *A Severed Head* (1961), *An Unofficial Rose* (1962), and *The Unicorn* (1963) are peculiarly unfulfilled, especially after the brilliance of *The Bell*. One senses that the author of these books is straining for the proper fusion of technique and vision. Despite its self-conscious emotional gymnastics, *A Severed Head* is perhaps the most successful of the three, for its comedy is sometimes one step away from terror. But again the failure is a failure of characterization. The characters are two-dimensional, so carefully patterned to fit the requirements of Miss Murdoch's satiric probing of modern love relationships that they never emerge as people.

"You cannot cheat the dark gods, Mr. Lynch-Gibbon," says Honor Klein, that dark-haired Jewess who springs

rhetorically full-blown from everybody's Lawrentian desires. But where for Lawrence flesh is flesh, for Miss
Murdoch it is narrative art and conversational lightness.
Still, there are some excellent things in *A Severed Head*
—the first person narration is reminiscent of *Under the
Net* and it is strikingly self-contained in the point of view
of Martin Lynch-Gibbon; the comic spoofing of psychoanalysis in the person of Palmer Anderson (known to the
patient he has seduced, Antonia Lynch-Gibbon, as "Anderson") is well handled; and the grotesqueness of a
world in which human relationships have been pretty
much reduced to confession as a substitute for instinct
is always apparent. In pursuit of freedom, Palmer and
Antonia are bound to a narrow, egocentric world, a
world that is experienced vicariously. Confession is good
for the soul—or so Palmer would have us believe. But the
novel, for all its wit and intelligence, falls down because
Miss Murdoch fails to establish true credibility for her
characters. We are left unconverted, and we are left unconcerned.

Miss Murdoch must be praised for merely attempting
An Unofficial Rose (1962). To ridicule romantic love in a
novel whose protagonist is a sixty-seven year old widower is
a stroke of conceptual brilliance. Unfortunately, there is
far too much else in the novel that is ill-conceived or not
carried off. And once again the reader's desire for credibility is imposed upon. Hugh Peronett is simply too im-
perceptive to have reached sixty-seven so successfully. He
knows, for instance, nothing about Felix Meecham's love
for his daughter-in-law, Ann, nor even about Mildred
Finch's love for him. Hugh's son, Randall, oozes so much
self-pity that we not only cannot sympathize with him
(which Miss Murdoch does not want us to do), we cannot
even believe in him (which she does want us to do). He is
dangerously close to caricature, and this in a novel which
demands very real and very solid people for sustenance.

But caricature seems to have become increasingly difficult for Miss Murdoch to avoid. Douglas Swann, the Anglican minister, is surely the dream realized of what every soap-box agnostic thinks Anglican ministers are. Felix Meecham is a straight-laced Victorian military hero; Ann Peronett is dull in her ideal English wifeliness; her daughter, Miranda, is far too precocious about divorce; and her nephew, Penny, is led like a lamb to the homosexual slaughter of Mildred Finch's husband. On top of all this, the magnet for Hugh's sixty-seven year old dotage, Emma Sand, is a rather decrepit goddess for so late an adolescence.

But there is much to be praised in *An Unofficial Rose*, just as there is in *A Severed Head*, for Miss Murdoch is simply too good not to win at least as much as she loses. The prose is extraordinarily precise and frequently metaphorically vivid. And her dry English irony meets its proper ground with these men, women, and children who live in a world strangely suggestive, for all its sexual painting, of Victorian England. The relationship between Emma Sand and Lindsay Rimmer is excellently handled, so that Emma succeeds as Randall's rival and conquors him through his own fear.

The novel's direction, however, is not really clear. In Hugh's selling of the Tintorretto so his son may have the opportunity to leave for Rome with Lindsay and to fulfill "his symbolic assassination of his father," we have a potentially brilliant insight. But it is not exploited. Despite the sale of the Tintorretto, we never meet the permissive amoralism with which the possession of great wealth endows one, as in Fitzgerald. For Randall, there is neither contempt nor pity; he bores us.

The Unicorn (1963) shares with *The Bell* a highly secluded world as its setting but little else. For where *The Bell* had been a brilliantly successful fusion of myth and reality, *The Unicorn* offers an artistic dead-end, myth manipulated by symbol, and both myth and symbol unfelt and unabsorbed. The terror in *The Bell* is real, its allegory successful. But the terror in *The Unicorn* is not real; catastrophe exists for its own sake; and the reader cannot enter its world. In a novel which is strewn with corpses, we are wholly untouched by death.

Once again, we have the war between illusion and reality; and once again, the human mind is the battlefield. Hannah Crean-Smith, imprisoned in Gaze Castle for seven years (in this, Miss Murdoch's seventh novel—of which every man can make what he will) under the watchful eyes of her husband's homosexual friend, Gerald Scottow, has been victimized by the illusion which permeates all life at Gaze Castle. Hannah believes that she is evil, irrevocably evil. But to escape her prison castle, the sleeping beauty must believe in the knight errant who is eventually to save her. Hannah believes only in her own evil. She plays with it, fondles it, adores it—and is adored for possessing it. She rejects the dedicated Marian Taylor, herself fleeing an unsuccessful love affair, just as she rejects the overwhelmingly self-conscious Effingham Cooper, to whom Hannah is "the castle perilous" toward which he "had all his days been faring."

But Miss Murdoch is trapped by her own ambition. Hannah Crean-Smith is neither demonic nor lovely; she does not feed us her terror because we find both her and her world so strikingly untrue. She is all pose, as is the world of Gaze Castle. Its bleakness, like her guilt, is told to us, but we fail to react. The burden of allegory proves to be an impossible burden; the sexual violence, which would have supplied the Marquis de Sade a moment of contemplative grandeur, is so unreal and so unfelt that the very grotesqueness of the novel is something the reader is aware of only as an afterthought. If the success of *The Bell* evolved out of the experiment of *The Flight From the Enchanter*, then *The Unicorn* strikes one as a distinct step

backward. Its allegory is meant to act as a mediating agent
for the novel; instead it chokes the characters so that they
are little more than articulations of points of view.

What partially redeems the novel is the final chapter,
which is devoted to Effingham Cooper. Effingham is still
immured from true suffering by what he himself acknowl-
edges as his "really fat and monumental egoism." After the
death of Hannah, of her husband, Peter, of Gerald Scottow and of Pip Lejour, Effingham's center of being has not
really been touched. And it is here, in his spiritual failure,
that the novel achieves some cumulative terror—here, not
in the actual deaths of Pip or Peter or Gerald or even
Hannah. Perhaps this is Miss Murdoch's true subject.
Perhaps we witness in *The Unicorn* a massive failure of the
emotions in which psychic masturbation overwhelms feeling.

One cannot call *The Italian Girl* (1964), Miss Murdoch's most recent novel, unfulfilled. It does what it sets
out to do and its Freudian trappings are a natural consequence of its author's increasing fascination with the ridiculous made sublime. Miss Murdoch is not among those
novelists who substitute Freudian theory for their own
perceptions in the hope that they can lend to their work
the semi-official sanction of modern psychoanalysis. *The
Italian Girl* is a Freudian novel but it does not lean too
heavily on Freud. The house is still Miss Murdoch's; the
trouble is that its furnishings are so sparse.

The novel deals with the discovery of self of one
Edmund Narraway, an aspiring saint in an unsaintly world
who becomes humanized when he returns to his childhood
home to attend his mother's funeral. Edmund is an en-
graver by profession and an ascetic by preference, a man
afraid of human contact and somewhat disgusted by the
fleshiness of the world; his brother, Otto, is a stonecutter
by profession, a drunkard and a lecher by choice, a man
who sees his own essence and the essence of all existence in

that very fleshiness Edmund finds disgusting. Both Edmund and Otto are what they are because of what they have come out of, and one immediately senses that the novel will be resolved through a reversal of roles—which, to a certain extent, it is. His mother's death serves as the road back to the past for Edmund, and it is through her death that he discovers the father in himself. It is his own father, the artist, the creator, whose spirit Edmund now finds in the house; it is as if, Edmund feels, "it was he [his father] who had just died."

When he arrives home, Edmund finds that he has been locked out of the house, a much too obvious way of telling us that he has been locked out of himself. He is admitted to the house by his brother's apprentice, a mysterious Russian Jew (Miss Murdoch seems, at times, to have become the victim of that aspect of Anglo-Saxon folklore which sees eastern and southern peoples as being somehow more sensual, e.g. the two Polish brothers in *The Flight From the Enchanter*) named David Levkin, who is offered to us as a symbol of life and as the lover of his master's wife, Isabel, and his master's daughter, Flora, possibly even of his master. Along with Flora, Isabel, Otto, David, and Edmund himself, Miss Murdoch's stage is peopled with two other important characters, David Levkin's prophetically insane sister, Elsa, who is Otto's mistress and watches the nocturnal dancing of the worms, and the Italian girl of the title, whose presence is, unfortunately, felt on a symbolic plane alone. It is she in whom Edmund is to find salvation, the last of the Italian girls who had come north in search of "a dream of strength." She is, as her name, Maggie Magistretti, implies, both prosecutor and judge; it is Maggie, not her sons, to whom the dead Lydia wills her legacy, and it is Maggie, not Isabel or Flora or even the mad Jewess Elsa, who is the novel's Eve. And Edmund, Miss Murdoch's fallen Adam, is saved by opening himself up to her, to life, to the south.

But Maggie doesn't work. She may be adequate as Eve, for Eve really has nothing to do other than to be Eve; she is not, however, very adequate as Maggie. And here we have a lesson Miss Murdoch might have better learned from Jane Austen than from Freud, what every major novelist seems to know instinctively—that character is fate. And fate is real, very real; it grows out of that we are, as Freud himself tried to show us, and it can be altered not by whimsy but by a true discovery of all the skeletons in all our closets. Unfortunately there is no true revelation of self in this novel; there is no more than a series of personality strip teases interspersed with dreams derived from textbooks, a love goddess sacrificed for love, and a generally much too stale symbolism which depicts sexual and emotional freedom in mysterious Russian Jews and Italian servant girls. The novel is like a glove that fits the hand too snugly; it is tight and smooth, but it is much too flimsy and easily stretched out of shape. In *The Italian Girl*, Miss Murdoch does make some attempt to control the growing predilection for fantasy that proved to be uncontrollable in *The Unicorn*. But the novel does not really signify a new breakthrough for its author; she does not commit herself to these characters and their problems. In fact, Miss Murdoch continues to insist on creating characters out of a world rather than a world out of characters.

Miss Murdoch has still not written the novel which *The Bell* seemed to promise. And one begins to suspect that she may never write it. For there is in her work a detectable failure of reality, a failure which seems to be growing as she indulges her taste for allegory and myth. To speak of her, as one critic recently did, as a novelist who seeks "to re-establish . . . [realism's] saner view of life" [1] strikes one as most questionable. It is difficult to understand exactly why Miss Murdoch is considered a realist at all; so much of her work falls into the realm of fantasy and her sources lie far more in fairy tale and myth than they do in nineteenth

century realism. And one also wonders exactly what constitutes her "saner view of life." Joyce Cary's world, for
instance, is ebullient, vital, and meaningful within the
contexts of our lives; it is sane and real, much more so than
Miss Murdoch's.

It is clear that Miss Murdoch is talented, but at no
point, not even in *The Bell*, is hers that overwhelming
talent which we associate with the truly major novelist.
What is lacking in her work is vision, the kind of vision
which Lawrence possessed in abundance. Lawrence is frequently an embarrassing novelist. Miss Murdoch never is,
partially because she is a novelist who confuses the thing
with the intensity the thing is meant to produce. And
nowhere is this more apparent than in her treatment of
sex. For all of its frequency, the sex in her novels is
fantasized sex, unreal and masturbatory, emotionally
voyeuristic. There are a few exceptions to this, most notably the sexual power Dora Greenfield asserts in *The Bell*.
In most of her novels, however, Miss Murdoch fails to
portray real sexuality, despite the great deal of sexual action in which her characters indulge. But action, especially
sexual action, should bring with it a sense of involvement;
rhetoric and purpose are not enough, as Lawrence should
have shown her.

The same failure of vision may be found in the violence
depicted in her novels. In a novel such as *The Unicorn*,
despite the violent deaths, the homosexual flagellation, the
barren landscape, the Gothic atmosphere, the reader is
simply not involved. For how can one be involved with
death and violence without feeling them. To excuse this by
saying that Miss Murdoch does not want "the reader to
feel awed" [2] is to avoid the issue. If she does not want the
reader to feel awed at death, especially at such violent and
destructive deaths as these are, Miss Murdoch had no
reason for writing the novel. When literature ceases to be
purgative, when it becomes an exercise in technique, then

it ceases to be literature. For if a novel does not force the reader to respond emotionally, even on the most elementary level, then it does not need to be written, certainly not as a novel. From her own Jake Donaghue Miss Murdoch should have learned that when we measure our lives by language alone, then we fail to measure them accurately. It is a failure of emotion, of involvement with the real and the human, which threatens to confine Miss Murdoch to a world stolen from the philosopher but never truly possessed by the novelist.

WIDMERPOOL AND "THE MUSIC OF TIME"

Charles Shapiro

ANTHONY POWELL, the ultra-urbane British novelist, is, by birth and choice, firmly and safely part of the Establishment. Residing pleasantly in Somerset, he can reflect on his schooling at Eton and Oxford, his friendships with both George Orwell and Evelyn Waugh, and, from a position on the uncommitted right, watch the changes in English society. Admired, paradoxically enough, by both the Angrys and their well-deployed enemies, his fiction is, in essence, the work of a cultured wit who is able to comfortably scan his own age. Best of all, he never goes beyond what he knows and feels. The territory of his twelve novels is, therefore, based on a world he understands and loves, and because he does not care so much, his humor has meaning as well as bite. Powell very well might be England's best comic writer since Charles Dickens.

Powell is chiefly known, of course, for his last seven novels, part of an ambitious cycle entitled A *Dance to the Music of Time*,[1] a work that will ultimately total twelve volumes. This remarkable project is an elaborate class comedy which explores the soul of modern Britain. Its popularity has been explained by Malcolm Muggeridge who feels we are now in an age when too little really matters. "Decaying societies, like decaying teeth, invite the tongue to probe, and touch the exposed nerve."

Powell's early probings were done in his five prewar

novels, which were, in a sense, finger exercises for his later, larger efforts.[2] In these extremely funny works there are twists to complicated plots, various oddballs chase one another about, clever lines are tossed off, and fatuous characters are displayed, observed, and caricatured. It is all quite delightful, and it is always useful to see pomposities steadily exposed, but there is a vagueness of focus which prevents the entertainments from becoming serious criticism. The laughs too often come a bit cheaply, are forced out of situations rather than characters.

All this changes with *The Music of Time.* Powell is working with a larger canvas, and his humor does not have to be sprayed about every page. He has set up as his narrator a man whose measure we are able to take fairly soon, an unpushy, sympathetic, vulnerable observer of modern England. Nicholas Jenkins' personal affairs are part of the interest of the books, but, more important, are his descriptions of the slow, often crazy progress of his friends as they move through schools, jobs, marriages, and, too often, through confusion. Behind their movements is an ever-present sense of history, of the two World Wars, the Spanish Civil War, and domestic crises, both financial and political. Fortunately, Jenkins has a superb, subdued sense of the absurd; it is this quiet laughter, however, which is, at first, a bit alien to American sensibilities, and it takes a while for us to tune in on his peculiar and *sui generis* attitudes. Once we accept Jenkins, and once we assume his interest in the ironies about him, we properly enter a fictional world where social comedy hints at private and public terrors.

Frank Kermode, noting Powell's style, wrote that "one felt the presence of something new and distinguished, a manner not only individual but potent enough to provoke involuntary imitation. For a while one saw people in a new way; they behaved like acrobats in a slow-motion film." [3] Now Americans are certainly not slow-motion people and most of our novels beat to a faster rhythm than Powell uses, but there is value in his intensive and reflective pace, in Powell's uses of time and coincidences to reinforce his intensive studies of how Nicholas Jenkins' friends react to a changing England.

A Question of Upbringing, the first of the *Music of Time* series, sets the architectonic structure for subsequent volumes, and many of the ironies and paradoxes in later books are based on the insights gained by Jenkins in this opening novel. Jenkins, from the outset, reveals himself as a man who continually evaluates past social adventures, who loves to hear gossip, and who too often sees life as a formal entertainment set up for his benefit wherein characters appear and reappear as if part of a large comic plan, a plan in which people seem to be manipulated for his pleasure. Nick, for large portions of the novels, stands at the periphery of the experience he recounts, occasionally darting towards the center, at times functioning as the hero, but repeatedly retreating to a safe distance to objectively reassess his own reactions to the events he narrates.

He has also thought a good deal about art, and many key scenes in the novels are deliberately set against statues and paintings in the background which serve either to reinforce or contrast the actions played out in front of them. This love and concern for art is developed at once as Jenkins recollects the scene by Poussin "in which the Seasons, hand in hand and facing outward, tread in rhythm to the notes of the lyre that the winged and naked greybeard plays." [4]

Nick goes on to be more specific about this symbolic dance:

The image of Time brought thoughts of mortality: of human beings, facing outward like the Seasons, moving hand in hand in intricate measure: stepping slowly, methodically, sometimes a trifle awkwardly, in evolutions that take recognizable shape: or breaking into seemingly meaningless gyrations, while partners disappear only to reappear again, once more giving pattern to the spectacle: unable to control the melody, unable, perhaps, to control the steps of the dance. Classical associations made me think, too, of days at school, where so many forces, hitherto unfamiliar, had become in due course uncompromisingly clear.[5]

As Nicholas begins his lengthy narration, reflecting on his adventures at a posh public school, we are immediately introduced to a major comic foil, Kenneth Widmerpool, a pathetic schoolmate whose blunderings, pratfalls, and sufferings are continually set against the progress of Jenkins and his more acceptable friends, Charles Stringham and Peter Templer. Later, in subsequent novels, as Widmerpool, still an arrogant fool, acclimates quite successfully to changes in English society, and as Jenkins' school chums come to trouble, the early school scenes take on added significance as a commentary on what Powell has termed the "awkward" dance of modern times. We wait, as Nick does, for the reappearances of poor Widmerpool, not only to laugh at his embarrassments but to acknowledge, as Jenkins is forced to with pain, that, in some curious way, Widmerpool's rise in the world can be seen as symbolic of a contemporary malaise, a contemporary failure of nerve and of judgment.

Widmerpool, the school patsy, is first observed (the year is 1921) going for "a run by himself." His sweat clothes don't fit, he is chugging away in a drizzle, and something "comfortless and inelegant in his appearance suddenly impressed itself on the observer, as stiffly, almost majestically, Widmerpool moved on his heels out of the mist." [6] The fates appear to have forced Widmerpool into schoolboy failure; for Nick recalls the boy's distressing resemblance to a fish, his high-pitched voice, his thick lenses, and, in general, his boyscout approach to a non-boy scout world. Widmerpool, it is evident, begins life as a victim; but there are hints, hints which multiply as the books progress, that his position in life will eventually change, that Widmerpool will, some day, be more than avenged for the miseries of a childhood hell.

Events during Widmerpool's school days foretell later happenings. His physical humiliations, for example, seem to recur on schedule. At school he is accidentally hit in the face by an over-ripe, skinned banana tossed by the heroic Budd, Captain of the Eleven. Budd apologizes, and Kenneth, with an almost "slavish" look on his face, waves off the gentlemanly apology. "It was as if Widmerpool had experienced some secret and awful pleasure. He had taken off his spectacles and was wiping them, screwing up his eyes, round which there were still traces of banana. He began to blow on the glasses and to rub them with a great show of good cheer. The effect was not at all what might have been hoped. In fact all this heartiness threw the most appalling gloom over the shop." [7] In later life, Widmerpool continues to be accident prone; what changes are his reactions to the humiliations, what remains is the continued sense of gloom he leaves about him for in a strange way slapstick is brushed with horror. And, as Widmerpool gradually obtains positions of authority and power, the basis for this horror becomes evident.

Widmerpool's sophomoric love life, dominated and curtailed by the woman he continually refers to as "my lady mother," serves as a steady contrast to the casual affairs and multi-marriages of many of Jenkins' friends. Self-centered, incapable of love or of any sustained sex life, Widmerpool concentrates on his career and his public image. Much has been written about the death of love in modern life; Widmerpool represents one aspect of this crucial failure. Stringham, Templer, and several other of Nick's acquaintances, without Widmerpool's concentration on career, fail in other ways. Nicholas, watching developments, learns a good deal that he can apply to his own affairs and to his own successful marriage.

Just as Widmerpool's futile efforts as a lover are paralleled in the intricate design of the novels with the lives of other protagonists, so is his rise as a successful businessman contrasted to the efforts of less fortunate men, ranging from Nicholas' Uncle Giles, the family parasite, to more ambitious failures. Though Powell's series is only one novel past the half-way mark, it is already evident that serious reversals of form have taken place. Those who bullied Widmerpool, who shunned and patronized him, now rely on him for favors and, to Jenkins' amazement, Widmerpool, once a figure of fun and loathing, becomes respected, honored, and feared. Widmerpool, in other words, becomes a point of reference for Jenkins and, by the time World War II comes 'round, Jenkins' future seems to be very much controlled by his former schoolmate.

A *Question of Upbringing*, divided into four sections, features Widmerpool in two of them, and even in this first volume we see a slow transformation. In the first part, chronicling public school days, Widmerpool is the victim, the chap to whom things are done. In part three, however, where Nick and Kenneth are boarding in France to brush up on their languages, Kenneth, still very much a buffoon, manages to interfere in the lives of fellow guests and begins to lecture Jenkins on matters of behavior. These lectures become a regular part of the rhythm of the novels.

"It is not easy—perhaps not even desirable—to judge other people by a consistent standard. Conduct obnoxious, even unbearable, in one person may be readily tolerated in another; apparently indispensable principles of behavior are in practice relaxed—not always with impunity—in the interests of those whose nature seems to demand an exceptional measure." [8] Thus, from the beginning, Jenkins gives special dispensation to fools. Meeting Widmerpool in France, Jenkins notes his "exotic drabness" and his "accusing manner." More significantly, in spite of Widmerpool's insignificance at school, "I still felt that he might possess claims to that kind of outward deference one would pay to the opinion of a boy higher up in the house, even when there was no other reason specially to respect his views." [9]

Widmerpool's views are on display in all seven novels to date, but they develop very little from his early philistine pronouncements. What changes is that his audience begins to listen and believe. When Nick first confides to Kenneth his dream of becoming a writer, Widmerpool expresses doubts as to the advisability of a career based on journalism or reading. "It doesn't do to read too much. . . . You get to look at life with a false perspective. By all means have some familiarity with the standard authors. I should never raise any objections to that. But it is no good clogging your mind with a lot of trash from modern novels." [10] And a few moments later: "Brains and hard work are of very little avail, Jenkins, unless you know the right people." [11] The right people, of course, at this early stage of Widmerpool's life, have not paid much notice to him. Soon they will.

Widmerpool forsakes college to go into the business world, Jenkins goes on to Oxford and, in a sour moment, recalls Widmerpool's strictures. "Perhaps Widmerpool had been right in advocating a more serious attitude of mind towards the problems of the future. I thought over some of the remarks he had made on this subject while we had both been staying at La Grenadìere." [12] There is always the frightening possibility that the Widmerpools in our lives are right, that they are our future. This possibility haunts Jenkins and becomes one of the recurring themes in *The Music of Time*.

A number of years after the summer in France, Nick meets Widmerpool once again, this time at a debutante dance. Widmerpool's appearance is a bit smarter, though "he retained that curiously piscine cast of countenance, projecting the impression that he swam, rather than walked, through the rooms he haunted." [13] Nicholas still visualizes Kenneth as a perpetual loser of footraces, and, quite improperly, is surprised at meeting Widmerpool at such a posh affair. Widmerpool displays equal amazement. "Good gracious, Jenkins . . . I had no idea you were a dancing man." [14]

The dance is the beginning of a long, involved evening. Widmerpool and Nicholas are both interested in Barbara Goring, suffering torments during the night on her behalf. For Kenneth it ends in embarrassment. Barbara, annoyed with his behavior, tells him he "needs sweetening," and in an impulsive action, constantly recalled throughout the novels, she shakes a large sugar castor over the poor man's head. Suddenly, after some unsuccessful shakes, the castor drops from its base, and the sugar deluges Widmerpool "in a dense and overwhelming cascade." The predictable "slavish" look, reminiscent of the adventure with the banana, appears on his face; and, once more, a general feeling of dejection comes over the viewers. [15]

Similar physical torments plague Widmerpool's social life; but, at the same time, his advancement in other areas is steady and at times spectacular. Attaching himself to Sir Magnus Donners, an important if not odd industrial giant, Widmerpool wheels and deals, and, each time he meets with Jenkins, the pattern remains; social inadequacy, business success; personal torment and public approval.

Sir Magnus Donners, "Chief" to Widmerpool, collects women and delights in teaching them "discipline" (and one can't help recalling fairly recent Tory scandals that shook and entertained us recently). Widmerpool is oblivious to Donner's perversions, though perhaps it is Widmerpool's own weaknesses that caused Donners to have him around. Throughout *Music of Time* the two men are presented together, often with Widmerpool arriving on the scene a bit late to serve as a living reprimand to the fun and games he interrupts. The contrast is remarkable, but there seems little to choose between the employer's obsessions and his employee's gloom. Nick enjoys watching both men on display, yet it is evident that he is becoming far more than a neutral observer of some strange behavior. What a man cares to watch tells us a good deal about him. What he cares to write about is possibly as revealing, for Nicholas, while supporting himself with the various positions open to writers in London, is, as he understands, a novelist, and he observes the hundreds of people he meets and describes as potential material for his fiction.

Jenkins is not only the protagonist whose character is betrayed, in part, by his reaction to Widmerpool. General Conyers, in a hilarious discussion of Widmerpool, analyzes his subject in a newly discovered, partly understood, Freudian and Jungian jargon. "It seems to me . . . that he is a typical intuitive extrovert-classical case, almost. . . . Looking back in the light of what I have been reading, I can see the fellow had a touch of exaggerated narcissism." Jenkins, slipping into the spirit of the psychological language, inquires as to whether the General believes a fear of castration might not be part of the trouble. "Possibly, possibly . . . Got to be cautious about that. You see this is how I should approach the business, with the greatest humility—with the *greatest* humility. . . . Can't help wondering about the incest barrier though—among other things." [16]

Gypsy Jones, at first appearance a rather typical bohemian girl who sleeps around a bit too much, seduces Widmerpool and then gets him to pay for her rather predictable operation. While the general is revealed as somewhat of an ass, Gypsy is seen as somewhat devious and certainly as cruel. Widmerpool's former schoolmates, bullies turned sychophants, display their essential weakness by their opportunistic behavior towards Widmerpool.

Other figures appear to go along with Widmerpool's

theories on life and personal advancement. An especially interesting example is Quiggin, one of a number of writers, artists, and musicians who follow the Widmerpool pattern. As Frederick Karl puts it, "Powell's 'new men' . . . push their way rather than swim along with the tide; and consequently they are traitors to their upper-class friends, whose code demands that no one work hard or accomplish anything." [17] Persistence, while vulgar, is seen by Jenkins to be rewarded; what Jenkins gradually understands is that this energy, mobilized by the Quigginses and Widmerpools, means more than individual success stories. It implies the failure of the upper-class to adjust to the needs of a new world. This failure extends *The Music of Time* beyond comedy, beyond the boundaries of cute social satire.

Once Widmerpool and his significance to the novels is established, his mere presence adds dimension to any scene in which he appears; one of Powell's favorite devices is to have Widmerpool enter at the conclusion of a piece of action, entrances which are often unexpected and quite often ridiculous.

Powell's novels feature a number of remarkable party scenes, and he is at his best when handling a group at play. For many of the characters in *The Music of Time*, partying comes naturally, be it the debutante dance, the bohemian brawl, or the more sedate dinner party; for Widmerpool it is an artificial situation to which he is not fitted. This has been fully established by the time Widmerpool blunders into the later moments of a dinner party given by Sir Magnus Donner. The result is one of the most unusual and striking scenes in contemporary fiction.

A number of important figures in *The Music of Time* are gathered at Magnus Donner's castle, Stourwater, described by Jenkins' wife, Isobel, as looking as if it had been made of cardboard. Jenkins, who had previous knowledge of the building, feels disappointed. "Now Stourwater seemed nearer to being an architectural abortion, a piece of monumental vulgarity, a house where something had gone very seriously wrong." [18]

Besides the Jenkins, the guests include Magnus Donner's current mistress, a multi-married lady, Anne Stepney; Jenkins' boyhood chum, Peter Templer; Templer's wife, Betty, who adores him but is extremely "dotty" and about to go insane at any moment; Hugh Moreland, a composer friend of Nick's; and Hugh's wife, Matilda, a former mistress of the host.

After the meal, during which the conversation hinged on affairs discussed in the first five novels, the host, famous for both his financial and sexual eccentricities, reveals his new hobby, photography, and proposes to photograph the guests. Tableaux are suggested, ranging from a history of the rise of Magnus Donners to scenes of Hitler and Chamberlain at Godesberg. Finally Jenkins, inspired by the large tapestries in the dining room which served as the basis for a good deal of table talk, proposes the Seven Deadly Sins, modern version. Utilizing flamboyant props available in the castle, the game is set up. Each posed group, featuring a different sin and a different guest, serves as symbolic reinforcement for many of the themes which appear and reappear in *The Music of Time*, and this, in turn, serves as a summary of the first half of the proposed twelve books.

Jenkins senses an excitement in the air, feeling that "the extravagance of the project offered temporary relief from personal problems, from the European scene." [19] The entertainment, however, does the opposite, bringing personal conflicts into sharper focus and even ending on a strong military note.

Moreland poses as Gluttony, Isobel as Pride, and Matilda as Envy. Betty Templer represents Avarice and her husband the three stages of Lust. During all these sessions there is a goodly amount of personal byplay observed by the fascinated Jenkins who, when his own turn comes, performs as Sloth. At the conclusion of the camera play, upset by Betty Templer's hysteria at the sight of her husband's posing with another woman, the door of the dining room opens. "A man stood on the threshold. He was in uniform. He appeared to be standing at attention, a sinister, threatening figure, calling the world to arms. It was Widmerpool." [20]

The sight of Kenneth Widmerpool in uniform "struck a chill through my bones." [21] He is presented as one more costumed figure. Jenkins observes that Widmerpool appears almost feminine with his Sam Browne belt, his cap, leather gloves, and predictable swagger-stick. Widmerpool, playing at being a soldier, has dropped by to consult with Magnus Donners on business matters. We feel by now, having been conditioned by Powell to see time and coincidence in his private way, that Widmerpool's appearance was inevitable. He just has to appear, and his appearance, while still a bit ridiculous, has taken on the form of the horror only hinted at in former moments.

Only one volume of the second half of *The Music of Time* has appeared. *The Valley of Bones* deals with Jenkins at the beginning of World War II, and we wonder about the possible shifts in his attitude towards himself and his country. After all, wartime tends to shuffle strangers together who normally would have no business with each other, personal dangers are faced, and values are reexamined in the light of new and often shocking events. If one is equipped, as Jenkins is, with a shrewd sense of humor and a quiet but perceptive interest in the pretenses of those about him, the troubled years might offer valuable materials for reflection. The forces that make for the new England are finally set in motion. England will never be the same; and Jenkins is there to observe.

Powell places his hero-narrator as a second lieutenant in a rather fouled up infantry regiment serving in Ireland and Wales. Intelligent as he might be, we are well aware that

Jenkins is far from being a born leader of men and even farther from being a spit-and-polish military chap. India would never have been won to be lost had the army been composed exclusively of clever fellows like Jenkins.

Of the assorted military types who pass over and beyond Jenkins, the most interesting is Rowland Gwatkin, his superior officer who loves his work for all the wrong reasons, whose own failure is as predictable as his commands. " 'A company commander,' said Dicky Umfraville, when we met later that year, 'needs the qualifications of a ringmaster in a first class circus, and a nanny in a large family.' " [22]

Jenkins' casual rhythm seems strangely unchanged by his initial army experiences, perhaps because he still refers events back to similar occurrences in former days. "All the same . . . it's a misapprehension to suppose, as most people do, that the army is inherently different from all other communities. The hierarchy and discipline give an outward illusion of difference, but there are personalities of every sort in the army, as much as out of it. On the whole, the man who is successful in civilian life, all things being equal, is successful in the army." [23]

Gwatkin, of course, has a good deal of the Widmerpool syndrome to him, but a second-string Widmerpool is not enough. Kenneth Widmerpool, the fool who gets ahead, arrives on the military scene at the end of the book. Jenkins is transferred to a new assignment. He knocks at the door of the DAAG, walks in and salutes; the officer has his back to the door and is dictating. "The DAAG's back was fat and humped, a roll of flesh at the neck." [24]

The voice, Jenkins notes, had assumed a Churchillian timbre, just as Gwatkin's addresses to the company "veered away a little from the style of the chapel elder, towards the Prime Minister's individualities of delivery." [25] When the officer turns 'round in his chair, it is, of course, Widmerpool. It is at once apparent that the former clown has finally emerged as something more than clumsy and disagreeable. "Various names were put forward within the division, yours among them. I noticed this. I had no reason to suppose you would be the most efficient, but, since none of the others had any more legal training than yourself, I allowed the ties of old acquaintances to prevail. I chose you—subject to your giving satisfaction, of course." [26]

Valley of Bones ends with the report that the German army is occupying the outskirts of Paris, and, as far as Jenkins' life is concerned, Widmerpool is in control of the home front. We await developments.

THE ECCENTRICITY OF
ALAN SILLITOE

Saul Maloff

THAT ALAN SILLITOE should have had so immediate and resounding an impact upon the contemporary British novel is as much a sociological as a literary phenomenon. In fact, he is a writer of limited resources—stylistically and imaginatively—and of limited thematic and dramatic range, so that his work, though it includes three novels and two volumes of short stories (the first volume of which contains the famous novella "The Loneliness of the Long Distance Runner"), seems composed of episodes in a single immense fiction that gains in intensity and comprehensiveness what it lacks in scope and variety. Save for *The General*, which in superficial ways appears to deviate from the pattern of his work, Sillitoe has been, from the outset of his career, the chronicler of working-class life in industrial Nottingham—the "permanent" working class on the edges of society.

The edges of society—that metaphor for the literature of alienation—has another significance in Sillitoe's work; and it is this difference which defines his interest for us—his distinctness from other writers of his generation—and accounts in some large measure for the attention he has attracted. Sillitoe is a throwback, an old-fashioned realist—in fact, a regionalist. He has attempted to make viable as art what was called, without embarrassment or sneering, the "proletarian novel" in the 1930's. His protagonists are profoundly rooted in their class, and draw such strengths as they possess – or come finally to possess – from that identification. This is, strikingly, not the case with the typical protagonist of the contemporary "picaresque" novel: whatever the picaro's origins, whatever his relation to society, he rejects affiliation, including class affiliation. He has opted out of the system entirely. In this central respect, Sillitoe is almost a solitary figure among the writers of the post-war generation.

Kingsley Amis may be taken as a representative figure of the neo-picaresque. There is a moment – the single moment in his work – in his second novel, *That Uncertain Feeling,* when after the shenanigans are all over, John Lewis ponders their meaning, only to feel deeply repelled by things in general and his life in particular. All for fun, he has sold out, thrown in with the enemy, the Anglican provincial upper class. To restore his sense of self, he leaves and returns to the working-class colliery community of his origin; and there – in a culminating scene which must have caused Amis extreme embarrassment – he experiences a kind of communion which we are left to feel is redemptive in its power. Critics have thought this inorganic, a false resolution of the novel, and its weakness; it is that – but for other reasons. It was Amis's last chance for significance. He took it; and what should have been an epiphany dissolves into a wish-fulfilling fantasy. His heart wasn't really in it; and, if one recalls his notorious talk before the Fabian Society on why he is not a Socialist, one will see why. After that, Amis settled for being what he brilliantly is: a very funny entertainer, perhaps the finest comic novelist of his generation. But for all the comedy of class and manners, Amis's protagonists are classless, deracinated, occupying ground that allows them a wide – though superficial – comic perspective.

Again, by way of contrast, consider John Braine's pedestrian novel of class *Room at the Top,* in which the provincial lower-class boy senses the chinks and cracks in a society somewhat more volatile now than previously—one that allows, within severe limits, some "upward mobility" for the most aggressive and ruthless. For Sillitoe, class is fate; the occasional Joe Lampton thrown up by the working class does not interest him—or interests him only as an object of contempt. Whatever else he is, whatever the elements of anarchism in his work, Sillitoe is obsessively concerned with a single idea, the discovery of self through the discovery—or discovery anew—of class solidarity. That egregious contemporary cliché—the quest for self-discovery—has no other meaning for him, and there is no other form which that process of consolidation, of cohesion, can take than the individual's recognition of his social role and class affiliation. The reader is struck again and again by the fact that when we enter the inner recesses of Sillitoe's protagonists, these are the contents we discover there. If the resolution appears sometimes confused and uncertain, it is only because of Sillitoe's own ideological confusions. The emotion is lucid, even if the mind is not.

Sillitoe's career corresponds with the rise in England of the "new left" (both as phenomenon and as periodical); and he should be viewed as a novelist in this context. The "new left" is neo-Marxist in orientation; Socialist in political affiliation (or, where unaffiliated, left-Laborite in sympathy); strongly anti-militarist—supporting, for example, a neutralist, unilateral disarmament position in foreign affairs. The movement is not to be found at any point in the political spectrum, but rather along a wide arc on its left from, say, Bevanite-Socialist to the "London anarchists" who played so prominent a role in the Aldermaston marches for nuclear disarmament. Once this context is defined, the force of Sillitoe's feeling, as it animates his characters, may be seen, not as aberrant or even idiosyncratic, but as representative of a strong current of thought and feeling in British intellectual and political life. The comparable American phenomenon is not nearly so influential.

These days, when "culture criticism" has become a major form of protest politics—indeed the politics at the "end of ideology"—the critique of culture, of the forms and quality of contemporary life, has come to be the prevailing method and mode of much of the best and most valuable writing of the new left. On the one hand, it has attacked the venal and debased corruption of culture by means of the mass media (see, among other works of this kind, Richard Hoggart's incisive study *The Uses of Literacy*); and, on the other, it has sought in the strangest places for vestiges of authentic working-class culture—a vigorous, truly popular culture that is possible to an organic community (see Raymond Williams' brilliant *Culture and Anarchy* and *The Long Revolution*).

In this realm of radical discourse, the key terms are *community* and *working class*. One of the animating historical impulses has led to some excellent studies of the sources of working-class politics, the most important of which is undoubtedly E. P. Thompson's *The English Working Class*, a book which is already a classic of its kind, and the finest work of historical scholarship since the great work of the Hammonds. Along with this form of scholarship, which is in part inspired by the desire to give back its history to the sector of the population generally neglected in the standard histories, there has been vigorous analytic study of all forms of the politics of protest in the English past, with especial emphasis on guild socialism, Christian socialism, and the various forms of trade-union ideology. Undoubtedly, the motive on the part of the new-left ideologists has been to give *form* as well as a historical past—to give, that is, *consciousness* to an English working class that stands in danger of losing its identity before the blandishments of (relative) affluence and debased mass culture. The working-class culture that Sillitoe describes is composed largely of cigarettes, the pub, and television. Arthur's father in *Saturday Night and Sunday Morning* lives out his old age in a coma of fags, beer and "telly."

Working in the failed tradition of the "proletarian novel" of the thirties, and carrying along with him echoes of Lawrence and Orwell, Sillitoe poses especially acute problems for literary criticism. The proletarian novel failed as art for many reasons (including the absence of talent in many of its practitioners), the most disabling being that it never really aspired to the condition of art, whatever its pretenses and proclamations. Before such a novelist even began to look at the life around him, he knew what it was like; before he began, he knew the end. The pamphleteers told him all he needed to know. All that remained for him to do was to provide confirming narrative. When we say that the novels and plays of the thirties were "didactic and tendentious," this is what we mean. They were slogans got up to look like literature. The present essay is not the place to fight again the literary wars of the decade of the Great Depression and the rise of fascism and the Spanish Civil War; but in considering Sillitoe it is necessary to record the catastrophic failure of what might conceivably have been a vital social art.

In a sense, then, what remained for Sillitoe as a novelist was a failed possibility. What he sought hardest to avoid (he makes clear from the first page of his first novel) is the heroization and sentimentalization of the working-class protagonist—Arthur Seaton in his first novel. He was helped in this enterprise by another, related "tradition," if that is not too grand a forcing of a term for so vastly different a pair of novelists as Lawrence and Orwell. In both—as in the post World War II new left—there is a hankering for the lost Eden of pre-industrial community, the prevailing sense of despoliation and fragmentation. Whether this is historically accurate or not is hardly the point: delusions can make good art, "truth," bad art. In the early novels of Lawrence, the machine brings the death of vitality—sexual and spiritual; and in such a representative novel as Orwell's *Coming Up for Air*, George Bowling seeks to escape the money-ridden squalor of petty-bourgeois life by returning to the arcadies of childhood—only to discover what he half-knew: that it does not exist, or exist any longer, if indeed it was ever more than fantasy. But "progress," he knows, has had a flattening effect upon him, as upon everyone. It is dehumanizing. All this may seem to the contemporary reader a mere restatement of the pastoral protest; but he would be mistaken to think so, for to do so is to miss much of the distinctive spirit of the contemporary novel, English and American as well as European. For the contemporary sensibility, the devastating process that the Romantics saw with great clarity has reached the terminus they dreaded. Alienation, anomie, reification—these may by now have become tiresome terms, so typifying are they of our discourse; but they are not mere words. They refer to real things and actual processes and denote measurable losses. To escape the bondage of the machine, which, while it provides him with fancy clothes and all the beer he can drink, nevertheless belongs to "Them," to the "rats," the "bastards," the bosses, Arthur takes out his bicycle on Sunday, after a wild Saturday night of carousing and goes out to what is left of the Midlands countryside—there to fish and restore his soul before the grind of the week begins again. Nothing would sound more fatuous to his ears than to talk of pride in work—that would be "their" kind of talk, hypocritical sloganizing devised to disarm and hoodwink, fourflusher's talk. What the guild Socialists meant by work fit for human beings has not been possible for a long time—and no one knows that better than Sillitoe's characters. You stay alive at the machine by dreaming of other things—women and gin and country Sundays. And always those dreams are crossed with nightmares of violence—Sillitoe's characters oscillate between their dreams of serene flight and their nightmares of entire desolation. From bullets and artillery, they fantasy with the most modern of weapons—thermonuclear in potency, megadeath in scope; but any weapon will do, for they are only extensions of the Luddite's spanner.

Yet to see this aspect of Sillitoe to the exclusion of others—as his critics have tended to do—is to miss the point of his work, and its peculiar relevancy. The "action," the motive, the force in Sillitoe's work which has the power to transform is not the ethos of "I'm all right, Jack," nor is it the black hatred which often seems the strongest emotion his characters are capable of feeling. (Compare the vigor of the writing when Arthur or Smith dreams of mayhem, with Arthur's erratic or listless feeling for Doreen or even Brenda.) The emotion, rather, is that of class loyalty—it would not be excessive, indeed, to speak of class love; and the general movement of feeling in Sillitoe's best and truest work gravitates from isolation to affiliation, from nonidentity to identity, from the sense of being man alone in a jungle (a recurrent metaphor in all Sillitoe's work) to the knowledge of being man connected, related to others not only by the fact of sharing a common predicament, but common joy and vitality as well. Despite all the swagger (and it is there to a sometimes irritating degree), all the self-conscious hardbitterness, all the display of cynicism, of having there before, Jack—despite, in short, the ferocious determination not to be taken in or to sentimentalize, Sillitoe shares with the novelists of the thirties, and in their different ways Lawrence and Orwell, a conviction of the superior virtue and aliveness of the exploited, the victimized. They may have nothing else, but they have one another; and they may not be saints (as the proletarian novelists were prone to make them out), but they have a kind of messy vigor, a sprawling amplitude, and the decency of those who work brutally hard for the little they have. "Maybe [Smith reflects in "The Loneliness of the Long-Distance Runner"] as soon as you get the whip-hand over somebody you do go dead." Sillitoe's workers have the whip-hand over no one; and if one should get it—should he "sell out," as Jack, Brenda's husband, does, simply by aspiring to become one of "Them"—he will go dead, and impotent; and Sillitoe punishes by cuckolding him. Virtue, if that is the word, is not personal; it is a class attribute, and it has to do with which side of the machine you are on, and how you make the readies.

To observe Sillitoe at his most characteristic, it is necessary to examine only some of his work; for with the exception of *The General*, altogether his least successful book, it is all of a piece. To date, his first novel is still his best; and of his shorter fictions, "The Loneliness of the Long-Distance Runner" is still his most effective, as well as his most representative. *The Key to the Door*, for all its flashes and bursts of fine passages and scenes, adds nothing to Sillitoe's stature as a writer that *Saturday Night and Sunday Morning* did not fully and vividly establish. And in his most recent book, *The Ragman's Daughter*, a collection of stories, Sillitoe is working the vein he has departed from only once (with unfortunate consequences) and in very much the same manner and voice. Indeed, if anything, the most recent volume is a regression if only because it represents no advance. Save for some moments in some of the collection's lesser stories, Sillitoe does here again what he did better in "The Loneliness of the Long-Distance Runner." The class war in "The Ragman's Daughter" is hardly more than a kind of hoodlumism with slight quivers of ideological overtones, and the apocalyptic fantasies of universal destruction seem willed and self-indulgent. The poacher of "The Ragman's Daughter" poaches simply because there are the rich and one poaches from the rich because—because they are *there*. And the boy who is in trouble over a stolen bike dreams of revolution, but his dream is a nasty boy's fantasy of revenge. The revolution of his fantasy is not cleansing or purifying; it is not the visionary's dream of a better world; it is more nearly a stormtrooper's quasi-erotic vision of holocaust—a day when everyone will be lined up with his hands out, "because mine won't be lily-white, I can tell you that now. And you never know. I might even be one of the blokes pickin' 'em out." It should be added, though, that these characters are declassed, aspiring out of their class. The "ragman" drives a maroon Jaguar; and his daughter visits her lover—with whom she breaks into factory offices for a lark—on horseback.

Where Sillitoe's work is least confused, it is possible to resolve a line of development—of growth—in his protagonists from mindless destructive nihilism to a sense of solidarity and communion. Nowhere in his work does Sillitoe give free rein to his fantasies of violence as he does in *Saturday Night and Sunday Morning* and "The Loneliness of the Long-Distance Runner," in the characters of Arthur Seaton and Smith; and nowhere does he so relatively convincingly portray their progress from their autistic nightmares to a settling—in which is their form of self-knowledge and their relation to others—to their class. The progress is uneven and fitful, as the thought of the characters is; but it *is* progress in the important sense that it defines the design of the fiction, and the author's intention. If they seem to stagger toward their end, it is (one often feels) because they talk too much (and this is Sillitoe's besetting sin as a writer as it is theirs as self-creators). But that is another matter.

Early in "The Loneliness of the Long-Distance Runner," Smith remembers an incident from his childhood. The memory occurs in the midst of a paroxysm of loathing—for "Them" and for all "Their" works and days. Memory gives rise to memory, image to image—and a strong current of feeling along an explosive fuse leading to a total detonation that will leave nothing standing. Images abound, spilling over one another in their fury—of biblical apocalypse, of class war, of actual war, of popular culture (in the invidious sense). Working-class Methodism and Marx and television and war movies run together in blinding confusion and rivers of blood. ". . . He whips out a knife and lifts it to stick me like a pig if I come too close. . . . [Smith fantasies] That knife is Borstal, clink, the rope. But once you've seen the knife you learn a bit of unarmed combat . . . and press back until he drops the knife." Smith, obviously, is a careful student of American television; and in some visceral sense he knows where he stands: "You see, by sending me to Borstal they've shown me the knife, and from now on I know something I didn't know before: that it's war between me and them. . . . I know who my enemies are and what war is. They can drop all the atom bombs they like for all I care: I'll never call it war and wear a soldier's uniform, because I'm in a different sort of war. . . . Government wars aren't my wars; they've got nowt to do with me, because my war's all that I'll ever be bothered about."

At that moment he remembers when he and his cousins went to the woods one summer day "to get away from the roads of stinking hot tar." They come upon high-school kids at a picnic, "a real posh spread out of baskets and flasks and towels . . . thin lettuce and ham sandwiches and creamy cakes"—a colliery kid's idea of paradise. They break up the picnic, scatter the fire, steal the food—driven by envy and the sense of exclusion. But remembering the act of vandalism three years later, from Borstal, Smith sees the "meaning" of the then meaningless act: ". . . those daft kids never dreamed that what happened was going to happen, just like the governor of this Borstal who spouts to us about honesty and all that wappy stuff don't know a bloody thing, while I know every minute of my life that a big boot is always likely to smash any nice picnic I might be barmy and dishonest enough to make for myself." Then, allowing himself a liberty very rare in Sillitoe's work, given his determination to avoid the merest hint of sentimentality, Smith adds, "Smith adds, "I'm not hardhearted (in fact I've helped a few blokes in my time with the odd quid, lie, fag, or shelter from the rain when they've been on the run). . . . If my heart's soft I know the sort of people I'm going to save it for."

Smith's sympathies are not ideological. A moment earlier he is thinking what he would do if he "had the whiphand." He would not "bother to build a place like this to put all the cops, governors, posh whores, penpushers, army officers, Members of Parliament in; no, I'd stick them up against a wall and let them have it, like they'd have done with blokes like us years ago, that is, if they'd ever known what it means to be honest, which they don't and never will. . . ." This is ideology; but it is the visceral basis of ideology. In Sillitoe, ideology skirts theory, has its source in the stomach and in the heart (and spleen); and he falters most as a writer when he gets too close to the mind.

Even, in a crucial passage in "The Loneliness of the Long-Distance Runner," when he informs us, glancingly, of his father's politics, Smith makes sure to hedge the information with irony. He presents his father not as a working-class martyr, but a passive victim of "Their" venality and brutality. He parodies his father's politics while honoring it. He and Mike are dividing the spoils of the robbery: ". . . all shared and shared alike between Mike and me because we believed in equal work and equal pay, just like the comrades my dad was in until he couldn't do a stroke anymore and had no breath left to argue with." Every detail in the long, crowded, garrulous story validates Smith's decision deliberately to lose the race, where to "win" is to defeat oneself and betray one's class, to say nothing of breaking faith with his dead father.

For some unaccountable reason, Sillitoe has been ill-served by his critics; perhaps, one suspects, because they have been so transfixed by the color and vividness of his literary language that they have failed to notice essential elements of his fictional strategy—or indeed where his meanings are to be sought. (Nor, listening closely, have they seemed to hear that his dialect, far from being "accurate," is actually highly stylized, mannered, "created"—in short, a *literary* language, for better or worse.) Not everyone failed to notice; and herein lies a parable which lights up important aspects of the British "new left" as well as the issue of art and ideology.

In retaliation for the loss of the race, the governor afflicts Smith for the six remaining months of his term with ceaseless humiliating work; but "it wasn't a bad life . . . considering all the thinking I did, and the fact that the boys caught on to me losing the race on purpose and never had enough good words to say about me, or curses to throw out (to themselves) at the governor." What is more, the pleurisy he contracted while running and in the subsequent six months of hard labor kept him from military service—which, in Sillitoe, is always a transcendent class victory—as not paying income tax is. Now the "logic" of "The Loneliness of the Long-Distance Runner" (as well as the novels)—where its force and pull lie, its "action" and direction—moves in one direction, Sillitoe in another. The logic of the story—its irresistible drive—is toward communion, toward class identification —else we have been misled by the author. In the final run, he is reminded again of "going back that morning to the house in which my old man had croaked" and he supposes that "since I started to think on these long-distance runs I'm liable to have anything crop up and pester at my tripes and innards, and now . . . I see my bloody dad behind each grass-blade in my barmy runner-brain. . . ." "All the thinking" he did in those final six months (one would suppose) had a great deal to do with the meaning of his victory-defeat and with the meaning of the "good words" the boys had to say about him—in short, with the meaning he has been pondering throughout his narrative. If this is so, then the resolution of the fiction, as Sillitoe wrote it, is false—is falsely portentous and sensational—a cheap and dishonest resolution. For, as it turns out, the "thinking" has been about ways of beating the cops, stealing and getting away with it, not making the mistakes he had made earlier. On the last page, Smith tells us of the big jobs he has pulled since Borstal—his form of revolutionary protest, of beating the system. And most embarrassing of all is the device Sillitoe uses to conclude. Smith gives the narrative he has written (the story itself) to a "pal" with instructions to try to get it published should he be caught. We hold the book; it has been published: either he has been caught, or he has been betrayed to the police by his pal, a "bloke" who would "never give me away" for reason of class loyalty: "he's lived on our terrace for as long as I can remember." In either case, as fiction, the conclusion is a dishonest trick.

One may surmise that Tony Richardson, the "new-left" film director who made the moving, lyrical film version of the story thought so. There is nothing in the film of Smith's subsequent career as a criminal; and even more important, there is nothing in the film of the kind of "hard labor" to which Smith is consigned in the story. In the story the governor has him "carting dustbins about every morning from the big full-working kitchen to the garden-bottoms where I had to empty them; and in the afternoon I spread out slops over spuds and carrots. . . . In the evenings I scrubbed floors, miles and miles of them." The governor punishes him, that is, not so much by *hard* labor as by menial, humiliating labor.

Richardson sought other meanings elsewhere—and projected them in the film's famous final moment; final frame, in fact. It is a "still" and beautifully imaginative cinematography. By some process the "still" is darkened, imparting to it a period flavor, like that of some old engraving—one that Blake or William Morris might have looked upon. Smith is not scrubbing floors or carrying slops. He is behind a workbench, at his machine, with the other boys. The governor is walking through the room with some visiting "bastard-faced In-laws." Smith, the worker at his machine among other workers at theirs, looks up and meets the eye of the governor. The still is held for a long moment—and the film ends. The end fulfills the logic of the film, projecting in other terms the meaning of the marvelous scene earlier in the film, where the boys, dying of boredom in the Borstal auditorium, suddenly come to life in a moment of ecstatic transcendence when in real communion they sing (from Blake) of building Jerusalem in England's green and pleasant land.

One further instance will suffice. The most vital episode in *Saturday Night and Sunday Morning*—certainly the episode most central to Sillitoe's intention—is not any of those that have been most frequently cited in critical discussion of his work. The novel is overwritten, or overspoken, and it is at times shoddily written, as is all of Sillitoe's work; but it crackles with vitality and is full of memorable scenes. Yet the center of meaning in the novel is not in any of the scenes that offer themselves most visibly to the eye and ear. And so vital does Arthur *seem*, with all his rage and fury, that it is easy to miss his essential nature—he is peculiarly lacking in vitality. He drifts, mechanically. He is listless. He does not respond or feel. He is altogether without emotional depth and resonance. He makes love, but he does not love. He drifts from "adventure" to "adventure," one more meaningless than the other. He courts, not women, but violence. He is a self-victimized victim.

The movement of the novel describes a progressive

running-down, and Arthur reaches bottom—the terrible awareness of the utter meaninglessness of his life—after the beating at the hands of the swaddies, the obligatory scene that ends the first part of the novel, the "Saturday Night" section.

At the beginning of *Sunday Morning,* Arthur is in bed recovering from the beating. The language that Sillitoe uses at this point is metaphoric in a way which recurs often throughout his work—a "Darwinian" language of tooth and claw, fang, and jungle. It is literary in the worst sense—affected, pedantic, "naturalistic," old-fashioned; and it is wholly convincing—as is Sillitoe's symbolic use of the fishing scene in the final pages of the novel. When Sillitoe is "literary," he is simply an inept writer living on unearned capital—Zola's and Dreiser's and Gissing's.

What is convincing here is the sense of absolute zero—Arthur's speechless awareness of utter meaninglessness, void, of the "thoughtless and unorganized way" in which he has been living. At the bottom, where it seems to him that "no place existed in all the world that could be called safe, and he knew for the first time in his life that there had never been any such thing as safety, and never would be, the difference being that now he knew it as a fact, whereas before it was a natural unconscious state." At this point he tried for a final time to cheer himself up in the old way: "Me, I'll have a good life: plenty of work and plenty of booze and a piece of skirt every month till I'm ninety." It is the old bravado, and it is followed immediately with the old fantasies of destruction—visions of men in big Black Marias coming down the street to smash all the tellies; his certainty "there'd be a revolution. . . . They'd blow-up the Council House and set fire to the Castle." But this time all the familiar rituals have lost their power to solace. When he taunts the cuckold Jack— "Yo've got your life an' I've got mine. Yo' stick ter your managin' and the races, an' I'll stick to the White Hoss, fishin' an' screwin,' "—the words sound strident and ineffectual, a whistling in the dark.

So on Friday night he goes home with thirty pound notes: bonus and wages; and on Saturday he buys toys for his sister's children and presents for the rest of the family. Then he goes to the house of his Aunt Ada.

Aunt Ada has appeared before, briefly in several scenes but always at strategic moments, in Arthur's progress—a resting place—in such a way that significance is made to attach to her which far exceeds the strictly *narrative* function of her appearances. As a character in a novel, she is a wholly sentimental conception—not so much a woman as a kind of working-class earth-mother, an emotional and psychic cornucopia. She is sprawling plenty actualized in masses of flesh—messy, disorderly, giving inexhaustibly of herself, surrounded by present husband and ghost of former husband, hordes of her children, grandchildren, children-in-law, animals—and her favorite nephew Arthur. When Arthur had early in the novel discovered that Brenda was pregnant, and needed to know about methods of abortion, it was to Aunt Ada—keeper of the secrets of birth and death—that he went.

To know and to be restored, he goes to Aunt Ada. Now he goes to be healed and made whole. The scene begins with a ritual solemnity, in a ceremony of giving, preparatory to the love-feast that is to follow:

> He pushed his way in through the defective back door and Aunt Ada launched into him because he had missed the mid-day meal, saying that now it was stone-cold in the scullery and fit only for the cats to eat. Arthur dipped his hand into his overcoat pocket and threw sixpenny bits to the children and gave cigars to Bert, Dave, and Ralph, so that the four of them filled the already warm room with clouds of smoke.

Immediately after that we learn that all day "Ada told Arthur, they had been expecting a coloured soldier from the Gold Coast"—a friend of one of her sons who is stationed in Africa.

Now, earlier, in establishing Arthur's nihilism, Sillitoe has made a point of remarking Arthur's indifference or hostility to politics. Concerned only with the pub, "fishin' and screwin'," Arthur couldn't care less what "happens in Kenya"—Kenya representing the whole wide world. And now, in the communion of Aunt Ada's house—in, let us say it, the "organic community" of the working class, its members bound together, not by money and the machine, but by love—now, into this symbolic home, presided over by that immense, inclusive, bountiful, mothering woman, corn in one hand, seed in the other, the Black African enters. The conception of the scene, and the redemptive power that it contains and confers, carries all the echoes and intentions of the "proletarian novel" of which Sillitoe is the inheritor.

That the scene itself is ineptly written need not detain us here. The design obtrudes. Characters move about in inert obedience to the author's dictatorial intentions, fulfilling his quota. Sam, it turns out, is one of nature's true noblemen. Race prejudice is exposed. The unreconstructed (if one may use an American term) are reconstructed or defected (literally, a character is knocked on the head). The women of the family kiss Sam or desire to. "Sam's like my own son," Ada exclaims. Hectic and turbulent, boisterous and violent, the occasion is a binding one. Feeling pours uncontained from its great source in Ada, in those who will never hold the "whip-hand." They are, as she is, magnificently alive. Her touch, and theirs, brings Arthur to life. At the end of the scene, he stands "feeling strangely and joyfully alive, as if he had been living in a soulless vacuum since his fight with the swaddies. He told himself that he had been without life since then, that now he was awake once more, ready to tackle all obstacles. . . ."

Arthur remains a "rebel," but he is now closer to being a

revolutionary. He returns to his obsessive theme—the factories, the labour exchanges, the insurance office, the bomb, the army, the "bastard government" : ". . . there ain't much you can do about it unless you start making dynamite." But he becomes Doreen's "young man"; and he will "lean his shoulder" against the "vast crushing power of government," and ignore or break "a thousand of its laws."

The intention of *Sunday Morning*, and of the novel, is reconciliation. To what? To an altered vision of life as humanly viable, as valuable. He can now, he tells himself, "for the first time" accept "some of the sweet and agreeable things of life." His "going-out" with Doreen is without the "danger that had tangibly surrounded him" formerly; and in the country he can be reborn weekly after the week-long death in the factory.

And there is the sustaining vision of the ancient life of coherent community poised against the anomic life of rapacious capitalism—as close an approach as Sillitoe will make to ideology, a kind of pastoral anarchism: "He remembered his grandfather who had been a blacksmith, and had a house and forge at Wollaton village." (His brother Fred, who in *Key to the Door* discovers the meaning of *his* life, and his class affiliation in the symbolic act of refusing to kill communist soldiers in Burma during the war, had taken Arthur to Wollaton village often, and "its memory was a fixed picture in Arthur's mind.") "The building—you had drawn your own water from a well, dug your own potatoes out of the garden, taken eggs from the chicken run to fry with bacon off your own side of pig hanging salted from a hook in the pantry—had long ago been destroyed to make room for advancing armies of new pink houses, flowing over the fields like red ink on green blotting-paper."

Now the memory has power to sustain, as does the furious reality of Aunt Ada, and the force that comes of knowing who you are and where you stand. For with all the anguish of war and slump and dole "it's a good life and a good world, all said and done, if you don't weaken. . . ." And, what is more, ". . . if you know that the big wide world hasn't heard from you yet, no, not by a long way, though it won't be long now."

Sillitoe is a historical surprise. In the utterly changed circumstances of the fifties and sixties, he has partially validated as art the "proletarian novel" of the thirties; and standing eccentrically against the current driven by his defter contemporaries, he has made possible a working-class novel.

C. P. SNOW:
THE UNREASON OF REASON

Frederick R. Karl

THE CHARACTERS in C. P. Snow's fiction operate according to a sensible plan or try to impose upon their world what they assume is a sensible plan. Unable to conceive of man's arrangements for himself as being so much confusion and chaos, Snow accepts what man has wrought as a form of order, not disorder, as pattern and scheme, not as accident or muddle. He sees the world as basically a projection of man's rationality, not as a manifestation of man's confusion and irrationality. He claims, further, that man's struggle with his self has been won—at least in part.

Neither Snow nor his characters would agree that man's arrangements are impermanent, a consequence of his fears, inadequate for happiness, and shot through with uncontrollable destructiveness. He eliminates soul-searching anxiety, or else submerges it deeply beneath his characters' public personality.

All this might be refreshing. One reads and feels untortured, somehow surrounded by people who seem vital and progressive, scientific, even liberal and decent. The key word is *progressive*—progressive scientific liberal humanitarianism, to give the attitude its full title. One suddenly sees the chance for progress, if people were to be like this.

Here are men trying to do their job well. Weak men, or flawed men, as the case may be, they are basically decent human beings sincerely struggling to overcome their short-comings in order to perform a useful function. Here are men willing to sublimate personal demons in order to live up to some common expectation. Here are men who believe strongly enough in their work—whether scientific, administrative, governmental, or political—to become captive to their job and its demands. These are men any mother would be proud of. True, they wish to get ahead, become recognized, even make money, but not at the expense of the public good. They may appear cynical and worldly, but they have a conscience and a knowledge of the rules.

Snow's view, acceptable as it may appear to those who accept it, is also very sad. For it is untrue and impossible, historically untrue and psychologically impossible. Men are not like this, have never been like this, and, short of being produced in test tubes, will never be like this. It's all a wishful dream—part of the illusions man holds about certain things so that he can continue to accommodate rather than lose hope in his kind. Such is the code of behavior that Snow's functionaries follow as they define England's role in the cosmos. The code is an illusion, just as it was in the nineteenth century. In the Victorian era, a "code" was derived to uphold a notion of progress and to disguise the fact that the Industrial Revolution might be plundering rather than aiding the English working class. The code, such as it is, is no more than a set of rules temporarily accepted, rules which exist to be broken as each man tries to fulfill personal ambitions and personal needs. Must we be reminded of this? In 1965?

Perhaps it was easier to keep up pretenses in the past, for then most men lacked the vocabulary to define what they must have suspected was true. Even so, many of the writers understood what codes and principles come to—especially public codes and principles. When Dickens wrote *Great Expectations*, he renounced the illusions, the romanticization, and all the simplifications. With one novel he leapt into knowledge. One need not, however, be a Dickens.

I have written elsewhere that Snow gives us a sense of how a modern man lives. I would strongly qualify that now. I indicated that he raises some interesting—and even crucial—questions about the nature of contemporary life. Moreover, he raises them in a different way from any other "serious" contemporary novelist. His reliance on reason, for example, puts to sleep many of those personal demons that writers for the last hundred years have traded upon; and his rational, courteous, somewhat formal human beings make it seem as if the entire world were upper middleclass English.

Snow's most recent novel, *Corridors of Power*, indicates how far he believes in reason, decency, and controlled ambition. Before reading this novel, one could still think that certain hidden demons perhaps counted in his work, that personal needs might preempt the public being, indeed that anxieties, doubts, and fears might one day transform the comic mask into a tragic mask and force a grimace into the face of the well-bred and impeccably styled Englishman. At least such possibilities lurked below the surface and occasionally manifested themselves in Sheila Knight, George Passant, and Roy Calvert.

All this, however, is deceptive. Snow is really not concerned with people. Instead he gives us a sense of the *things* that exist in the modern world. His is a universe of events, happenings, circumstances, situations, conditions —all those aspects of life which can be given a final solution. It is by no means fortuitous that the fortunes of Roger Quaife (in *Corridors of Power*), a young Conservative member of Parliament, depend upon a vote. What could be more clear-cut and final? The eventual decision will be in the form of a number, so many on this side, so many on that. What a progressive, democratic, even scientific way to resolve an issue!

This way of treating *things* is carried over to people: the vote for a master in *The Masters*, the vote to exonerate Howard in *The Affair*, the vote I just mentioned in *Corridors of Power*, the "vote" on George Passant which leads to his rejection as a civil servant in *Homecoming* and to his acquittal for fraud in *Strangers and Brothers*, the vote on Roy Calvert's election as a Fellow to a Cambridge College in *The Light and the Dark*, the administrative decisions in *The New Men*, and so on through the many major and minor decisions in all nine novels.

A vote or something akin to it is a way of deciding things in social terms, a method of evading the individual's own conclusions. Given Snow's purpose in the entire series of *Strangers and Brothers*, perhaps this numerical resolution is inevitable. Snow's plan is to measure men against a world they must in some way control even when they disagree with it. They must be mature, courageous, and capable of overcoming petty ambitions in favor of the public good. In *Corridors of Power*, for example, Roger Quaife takes a public stand on nuclear development in England that can—and does—compromise his career, all this despite intense personal ambition. Lewis Eliot himself, Snow's ubiquitous and flat narrator, admires Quaife's decency, even though Eliot votes Labor and Quaife is a Conservative. Within the world of mature men, Eliot is able to admire principle and decency, clashing political views hardly ever becoming a factor. Snow appears anxious to close off all differences, or to demonstrate that differences are rarer than similarities. Eliot always "sees" the other side, and even understands it. His very impartiality makes him admired; he is considered safe as well as sound, twin virtues in Snow's iconography.

Despite Snow's modernity and liberalism, there is a good deal of English stiff upper lip, a strong sense of clubiness (much is made of being "in" and being "out"), and an implied tone of the white man's burden—without of course any racial connotation. There is a world "out there" (Russia, the United States, Whitehall, London) which must be confronted; there are significant decisions (nuclear bombs, elections of Fellows and Masters, civil administration appointments) which must be made. There are, in addition, high level meetings at which each official must have all the facts impeccably assembled, or else face humbling defeat, perhaps even lose a rung on the civil service ladder. The new gods of the twentieth century perform few hieratic functions; rather, they judge one at administrative meetings, faculty committees, and government hearings. These gods take the form of Hector Rose or someone like him, whose own position depends on making the correct decision at the right time, trapping others without himself being caught. Administrators now form England's thin red line.

The reader is always amazed at the long hours Snow's characters keep: day-long jobs requiring precision and presence, followed by public functions, large dinner parties, long political or scientific discussions late into the night, succeeded still further by cabals, caucuses, and endless discussions of strategy. The next day finds more of the same. When do these people read, write, work out their problems, make love, keep up with their "fields"? Are there any hours of reflection and meditation? Any attempt to think through the entire system in which they are involved? Is there ever recognition of what fools they are dealing with and any realization of what utter fools they are themselves for taking seriously what should be mocked?

These are valid questions, for Snow accepts this kind of world and at times admires it. In this respect, he is unique among novelists who ask to be taken seriously. He assumes that work is more significant, certainly more interesting, than the man himself. One must get the job done whatever the cost in human effort. We can say that his postulate of human nature is Euclidian—the parallel lines of the public and private man will never meet.

There is in Snow the sense of dedication of the scientist in his laboratory, first charted in *The Search* (and there superficially repudiated), then pursued in *The New Men* and elsewhere, and finally carried over into his whole view of life. He has perhaps considered the psychological loss that takes place in a man as a consequence of concentrating on the job to be done, and after consideration has decided that the loss is worth the candle. Seen this way, one can better understand the ferocity, although not the indiscretion, of F. R. Leavis's attack.

In Snow's view, there is little sense of *being*, or whatever one chooses to call it. Man's "courage to be" is transformed into his need to work. This may be partially true as a diagnosis of modern man, but it is surely nothing to applaud. Snow praises man's ability to sublimate his inner being in favor of his outer role, and this too is hardly commendable. Such a repudiation of identity should be a source of grief, not celebration.

As still heir of the Romantic tradition in literature, the modern novel has to be concerned with what man has lost, is losing, and will come to lose. To be concerned solely with what man is doing—how he is working and how he gets ahead or falls behind—is to assume that nothing has changed in the last 175 years. Such an assumption is strange coming from a man who was once at the forefront of nuclear physics, a man interested in limning contemporary character and mores for a modern audience.

Literature must go against everything that is comfortable, settled, and arranged. It must seek some kind of order, only to upset it. And it must always, within this controlled chaos, assert man—whether he is good, bad, or indifferent. There is no moral value one way or another in man's ability to do a job well or in his ability to function correctly in society, unless what he does is meaningful to him. We are talking about literature, not sociology, science, or history. Aristotle made the distinction 2300 years ago. He was talking about men and not institutions. The rest is dishonesty.

The only literature that is possible at present is one in which hate and disgust are present or potential. There are too many things to hate, both within and without, for the serious novelist to offer reconciliation, love, devotion, or faith—no matter how difficult and torturous he makes the resolution. As long as certain traditional values were generally acceptable, the need to hate was not paramount. The feeling, in fact, could be contained through some kind of belief, whether in God or in self. With such values no longer viable, a literature of hate is the sole way—hate, that is, transformed by satire, irony, or some other form of wit. Direct and exposed hate aimed at a particular group or idea is, of course, no more effective than uncompromised courage or "honest compromise," what Snow calls mature judgment. Of recent fiction, I have in mind Günter Grass's *The Tin Drum* and all those lesser novels of the absurd which deal in hate transformed by irony and satire into moving documents. The modern novel must celebrate unbelief, not try to find a solution for it.

No matter what our honest concern about nuclear warfare, the outcome of racial issues, the power struggle between East and West, the nature of national defense, or the success and failure of democratic processes, the chief issue must be: How does man confront *himself?* This is not to assume that soul-searching will be sick or neurotic or self-righteous. It does mean that only inner order counts: how man recognizes his need for order, how he faces the conflicts between this need and his basic desires, how he comes to terms with the tensions that develop as he slowly attempts to gain some order, and finally how he accommodates the kind of order, both within and without, that is uniquely possible for him. In Grass's novel, Oskar Matzerath's Tin Drum is his ironic attempt to impose personal order on a chaotic situation and at the same time gain further knowledge of himself. So too is his refusal to grow, as well as his ability to shatter glass with his voice. Grass suggests that the barbarity of Nazi Germany becomes meaningful only if the situation is seen absurdly. Then nazism gains reality not simply as an historical movement but as a way of life broken down into individual experiences.

All this may seem to be too much to ask of a modest writer like Snow. But when a novelist attempts to deal with large events on a large scale, as Snow does in many of the novels in the series, then his ambitions call for commensurate criticism. If a writer is to handle contemporary life, then he must do so with contemporary awareness and contemporary techniques. Only literature can make some sense of political maneuvering and public policy, things which the newspapers and magazines have so distorted that we no longer pay attention. When a novelist deals with such material, as Snow does in *Corridors of Power*, we expect something different from what the newspapers report. The novelist must present a point of view that is always *more* than the point of view of any of the participants. Obviously he cannot see them as they see themselves. The novel must have sufficient invention to make credible the fantastically involved motives and intentions that go into politics. Policy very often is not the result of planning but the consequence of a ruler's needs—whether we speak of a democracy or a dictatorship.

Let me give an example: During Eisenhower's eight years as President, it occurred to many good Americans that U. S. policy was being formed on the golf links and that certain decisions were reached over others because they took up less of the President's time. It appeared, further, that as the President became a better golfer—that is, came closer and closer to par for a given course—he would have commensurately more time for public policy, whatever the results of that might have been. If the President eventually became an expert golfer, we thought, then we could feel assured that national interests were gaining more of his attention, and therefore all our political hopes were focused on the improvement of his game. A hole-in-one for the President might mean more medical care for a hundred families, or better housing. An eagle or a birdie could lead to less tension with the eastern bloc. A bogey, on the other hand, might necessitate late afternooon practice on the White House lawn while Negro schoolchildren ran the gauntlet of jeering whites and Texas oilmen found loopholes in the tax laws.

Such considerations may seem absurd, and yet the nature of politics calls for some kind of absurd expression. To approach nuclear policy, the principles of the English Conservative party, and the Suez issue in the spirit of decent men trying to work out decent solutions is to lose sight of what all this means. In the process of showing how decisions are made, Snow omits significant details and fails to suggest the overall absurdity of each man's efforts. What pompous fools these administrators and scientists are as Snow describes them, and yet he takes them seriously. What dishonest men they really are behind his somewhat pious reminders that all men are a little frail but nevertheless do the best they can. It is not a question of how well they do—with that as a measurement, we should prize termites, for gram for gram they work harder and plan better than man—but a question of what goes into the work, into the planning, into the intentions of the man. Then we can see that public policy is as much a part of personal neurosis as it is something consciously planned. Perhaps all history is neurosis, as Norman O. Brown tries to persuade us in *Life Against Death*. This is not such a new idea: the good novelists have always suspected it. Tolstoy rejected fiction because he saw where it was leading him.

The novelist must plunge into the very worst of man without any guarantee that he will come up with something positive, and certainly not with solutions. A writer begins with this kind of honesty. It has been one of Snow's virtues that he accepts man's imperfections, but he is unable to follow through. In fact, quite to the contrary, his somewhat jaded analysis of man gives way to an obsession with man's job, the sense of work satisfactorily attacked and completed, the fulfillment of a task that everyone assumes will be carried through. Snow is too anxious to see results, as though only results count in the making of a man. In this respect, when has a central character been more anal than Lewis Eliot? He retains everything that he hears and sees, he refuses to give anything away, and he squats patiently while blows reign upon his shoulders and head. His tight bowel blocks off parody, satire, and all other forms of wit. When he squeezes, piety is emitted, and when he grunts, only air, not substance, emerges.

Public roles—the sum and substance of C. P. Snow's world—ultimately become meaningful to us only as they reflect private beings. The novelist must recognize that man has many faces, only one of which he wears in his work; and that the face at work is often the least, not the most, interesting. The burden upon the contemporary writer is immense. At one time in the history of the novel, a broad view of some kind, the ability to create character from the outside, a verbal facility, a sharp eye for detail, and a tolerant humor were sufficient to create fiction of some worth. No longer is this sufficient. As a genre becomes more sophisticated—and in two hundred years the novel has become as sophisticated as poetry in two thousand and the drama in three—we expect more and more from it. The novelist must use the tools of past masters and still be flexible and adaptable enough to identify the sands of time as they run out. He cannot hide anything, and he cannot hide behind anything.

The perspective for the contemporary novelist must be

rooted in some form of irony. Contemporary life is over-whelming, not solely because it is the only life we know intimately but because we have lost all the certainties. The novelist cheats who writes as though certainties were still possible. They are not and cannot be. Instead, he must show how man faces uncertainties and tries to find some order by which he can live in himself. The straightforward presentation of the naturalist and realist is no longer work-able. A Dreiser, a Lewis, and a Zola have done their work, and done it well. Snow, unfortunately, has tried to be the naturalist of the contemporary scientific and political world, and when we measure his achievement at its best—as in *The Conscience of the Rich* and in parts of *The Masters* and *The Light and the Dark*—we see that even here his regard for tradition, for continuity, and for the amenities blinds him to the real nature of man and the real issues. Were he able to come to grips with these, then his naturalistic-realistic approach would no longer suffice for him and he would have to confront the very absurd world he has so often deplored in modern fiction.

MURIEL SPARK:
THE SURREALIST JANE AUSTEN

Charles Alva Hoyt

IN 1957 a remarkable first novel, *The Comforters*, appeared, swollen with every sort of excess: exuberance, flummery, treachery, witchcraft, smuggling, fanaticism, thievery, madness, magic, irony, death. The literary world was overwhelmed, carried quite off its feet. As one reviewer said later, "I cannot quite see how it was done, but the transformation of Muriel Spark from a minor poetess into one of the most distinguished novelists writing today is a remarkable literary phenomenon." Mrs. Spark's metamorphosis was superficially at least as dazzling and as quick as the movement of her own fiction. Unlike Byron, however, another poet whose life the critics sometimes confuse with his art, she did not awake one morning to find herself famous. For all her easy conquest of the reviewers, her reputation among the general public has been moving at a measured pace, from mouth to mouth as new readers discover her. She gives the curious effect of being one's own personal property; surely, one thinks, a talent so unique cannot appeal to the mass audience. Such snobbery to one side, it is right and proper that Mrs. Spark evoke an Augustan response. For despite her Byronesque feats among the critics, despite her exuberance, flummery, madness, and magic, she has little of the Romantic about her. No matter how the plot may rage, or the characters threaten, even though reality itself totter on a ledge, the reader is conscious of the cool, clever female mind in control. This level scrutiny from the distance plays continuously though mildly upon every frenzied human action like the soft, semi-contemptuous gaze of the household cat. Muriel Spark is ever the reasonable recorder of unreason: she is the Jane Austen of the surrealists.

This is the first and perhaps the foremost challenge of Mrs. Spark's art: the assessment of its unique but elusive quality. And the key word in this assessment is, I think, mischief. Mrs. Spark is a thoroughly mischievous writer. By that I do not mean only that she plays tricks upon her characters—although she does—or upon the reader—she treats him even worse—but that she also views the universe itself as mischievous. The cosmos is neither void of all sense, nor is it sentient but preoccupied: it is both aware of individuals and fond of meddling with them for its own amusement. It is, in short, mischievous.

The classical application of this concept is best seen, perhaps, in the Greek drama. The immutable order of things has played a cruel joke upon Oedipus, which he may neither understand nor avoid. To attract thus the attention of Fate—the convenient word for the will of the universe in its playful application to individuals—is what is to be most avoided, as countless minor figures tell us. "I would like to be safe and grow old in a humble way," the nurse in Euripides' *Medea* says; "Greatness brings no profit to people."

The cosmic joke is fleshed out in irony, always a godlike prerogative. Tasting irony is nothing more than experiencing life at several levels simultaneously, which Gods must do, and audiences may do, as when Clytemnestra, defending herself against charges of adultery, says, "I know no pleasure with another man, no scandal, / More than I know how to dye metal red." But it is only the characters in the drama, not the spectators, who do not reflect that there is indeed a way of dying metal red, and that Clytemnestra is shortly to avail herself of it.

The severely classical approach is rarely found in Mrs. Spark's writings. One notable exception is "The Go-Away Bird," a work of medium length which, if considered a short story, must be called her best. Formal in design, it takes up a South African girl of good family and sees her through a short and empty life to her predestined end, a murder prompted by no act of her own. She is shot by a man whom her uncle had wronged; but both "wrongs" are of nebulous character. Was it wrong for Oedipus to defend himself? No, that was not the crime itself, but only another symptom of the coming vengeance. The crime had never been in his hands. Daphne du Toit is no more guilty than he; and even the original crime of her uncle is no Thyestean outrage, but a poor lapse into a community fault—a fondness for someone else's wife. This time, however, the often insulted husband is determined to be revenged. From the beginning it is clear that he will kill Daphne, but he does not manage to do so until his extreme old age, when he is too senile to know what he has done. Daphne's unhappy life is stopped by a reflex action.

Aside from this final stroke, the irony is constantly at work in the story through the agency of the Go-Away bird, which screams its message at Daphne in vain. Its voice is echoed everywhere: by her swindling English landlady, her parakeet, the man she thinks to marry. But there can be no flight. As Daphne's friend, the alcoholic Donald Cloete, puts it, "I grant you we have the natives under control. I grant you we have the leopards under control. . . . We are getting control over malaria. But we haven't got *the savage in ourselves* under control." Futile enough, from him, and perhaps reminiscent of *Heart of Darkness*, but true, and in context, just. There is no sure way of escaping the wit of the cosmos; but moderation, humility and common sense are man's best hopes.

Mrs. Spark's universe, however, does not always demand blood sacrifice. Like that of the Greeks, it reveals its playfulness in an almost continuous flow of irony, but it is quite as fond of comedy as it is of tragedy. There is furthermore in her work an almost irresponsible impertinence towards everyday reality that is, however refreshing to the reader, totally foreign to Classicism. Thus the heroine of *The Comforters* is disturbed to overhear the author making the novel out of her misfortunes. That is a technique beyond irony, one which owes something to the opposition. Although she is not a Romantic, Mrs. Spark is perfectly willing, like every other modern writer, to accept some of the advantages secured by Romanticism, principally those implied in the postulate that individual experimentation is equal or superior to observation of the most correct models. Her chronology, for example, is highly inventive, and becoming more so—her most recent book, *The Girls of Slender Means*, is her most experimental in this area. Her repeated outrages upon probability, while individually not hostile to the classical tradition, have nevertheless a cumulative effect which is distinctly unorthodox. Let us think again for a moment of *The Comforters*. It would not be surprising to read of witchcraft in a play by Racine, for example, nor would we find death out of place there, nor thievery, madness, religious fanaticism, sorcery, treachery. When, however, all these are tumbled together in one piece, along with several other ugly human preoccupations, then for a comparison from the drama we are forced to go to Thomas Kyd. Her material can upon occasion be described only as sensational: *Robinson*, for example, has two men and a woman marooned on a small island with its ordinary inhabitants, a man and a boy. Presently this man, the island's owner and ruler, vanishes in a welter of blood-stained clothing, leaving the rest behind to suspect and waylay each other.

Much more to the point than her subject matter, of course, is her approach, her style. And while it is undeniably Augustan in its principal tendencies, it has its romantic characteristics, too: it is aggressively inventive, as mentioned above; it is occasionally flamboyant and melodramatic, as often in the novel *Robinson*, and best of all, it is infiltrated with a perverse but delightful zaniness of echo and chime that is part form, part content.

From *The Ballad of Peckham Rye*:

> Dixie said, "He's common. You only have to look at his sister.
> Do you know what Elsie did at her first dance?"
> "No," said Mavis.
> "Well, a fellow came up to her and asked her for a dance. And Elsie said, 'No, I'm sweating.' "

Several pages later a character is trying to buy cheese, and the other customers are protecting him from the grocer: " 'Don't you give him that,' said the Young Woman, 'it's sweating.' " Coo, says the charwoman in *The Comforters* wonderingly, and Coo, responds the pigeon in the next paragraph. And then everyone can read everyone else's mind. From *The Comforters*:

> "To think that our old trusted servant should do a thing like this."
> He thought that a bit of hypocrisy—that "old trusted servant" phrase.
> "You think I'm a hypocrite, don't you?" his mother said.
> "Of course not," he replied, "Why should I?"

All of this and a great deal else—witchcraft, miracles, seances—is presented in a beautifully offhand way, as if describing the most prosaic part of the daily routine. A certain obnoxious woman, roundly damned and wished elsewhere by everyone, literally disappears. Lovers send each other identical telegrams, to their great terror: "Come immediately something mysterious going on." Death calls on the telephone. Flying saucers come in the window. Seraphim appear at amateur theatricals. All the events of everyday life shade off imperceptibly into the incredible. As in Dali's pictures, the household effects are clear and recognizable: the wristwatches are wound and ticking—

but they lie limp over a chair. The meticulous ironic intelligence of the Augustan observer presides over a world which has proceeded one step beyond reality.

This rather curious duality is at the bottom of all of Mrs. Spark's novels and stories, as we shall see. What sort of mind would express itself in such terms? Perhaps one which, too vividly conscious of the vast riches of mystery in the universe, and only too well convinced of intractable and meddlesome forces at work among us, seeks to keep them and itself under control by assuming a pose of Neo-Classicism, with its valuable disciplines of irony and detachment. Some of the finest writers of the past, notably the eighteenth century, give the same impression: Swift, for one. This hypothesis finds support in many of Mrs. Spark's favorite themes—for example, that of conversion to Roman Catholicism, which occurs again and again in her work. I am not speaking of the universal concern of men, writers or otherwise, to give rules and meaning to mystery and chaos. What we have here is something different: not the scientist's or the theologian's attempt to reason the demons out of the thunderstorm, but the magician's effort to make the demons do his bidding. For all her Augustan manner, Mrs. Spark understands that the artist traces his descent from the sorcerer, and, taking advantages of the proper safeguards, she is willing to act on her knowledge.

She has been compared with good reason to a number of writers: V. S. Pritchett, Anthony Powell, Angus Wilson, Ivy Compton-Burnett. I should like to suggest a couple of new comparisons. First, in her dealings with the fantastic, in which she far exceeds the writers just mentioned, she comes near another great expounder of the playful universe, the late Isak Dinesen. Both women are formidable stylists, both are superior storytellers, and both are gifted with a superb sense of the grotesque. Elsewhere, to be sure, the parallels are not so neatly drawn; Miss Dinesen is a strong Romantic whose characteristic style catches something of the high seriousness of the heroic folk-ballad, or its more successful imitations, like *The Rime of The Ancient Mariner*. Then too Mrs. Spark has none of her historic sense, that brooding preoccupation with the past which is the wellspring of the Gothicism with which Miss Dinesen has identified much of her own work. With all that can be said of their differences, however, there remains the fact that they very much agree upon one fundamental principle: a full acceptance of the mystery of life.

Secondly, Mrs. Spark it seems to me owes something to that gifted although sometimes patronized group of women who have raised the mystery story to such a peak of perfection in our time: Agatha Christie, Dorothy Sayers, Josephine Tey and Ngaio Marsh, to name some of the most prominent. Surely their influence has been widespread, and in what areas if not precisely those in which Mrs. Spark excels: ingenious, guileful construction and nimble unreflective style. A simple check of Mrs. Spark's plot-lines shows the affinity, and a strong one it is: *Robinson*, fraud and attempted murder; *Memento Mori*, blackmail, murder, and intimidation; *The Ballad of Peckham Rye*, alienation of affections and false pretenses; "The Go-Away Bird," murder; "The Portobello Road," murder; *The Bachelors*, forgery, fraudulent conversion and attempted murder. One can go on and on, classifying each work according to its dominant crime.

The Comforters provides so many that it is difficult to know which one to start with. In other ways, too, Mrs. Spark's first novel is generous: it offers up her themes and preoccupations, her favorite characters and techniques in unequalled profusion. If not her best novel, it is certainly her broadest. And it is good, too, very good, this careening account of an unstable novelist, Caroline Rose, and her religion, her lover and her friends. The lover's old grandmother is a diamond smuggler: crimes in the book, smuggling, sorcery, theft, blackmail. The last may be stretching it, but there are no certainties in the world of Muriel

Spark. I may be wrong about the heroine; at the ending there is some indication that the novelist Caroline Rose and the novelist Muriel Spark are literally one and the same, and that the heroine is someone else—specifically, the diamond-smuggling grandmother. At least it is she who gets married, when the villain dies and all the other strings are gathered into a neat bow-knot.

Novelist or not, Caroline provides the book with much of its power: thin, good-looking, intense, capable of enjoying sex but not marriage; a convert to Catholicism, she is an obvious persona and the first of a long line in Mrs. Spark's fiction. It is here, however, that she is acknowledged openly as the book's author—another bonus provided by the first novel. Her lover Lawrence is one of Mrs. Spark's better men. Just as most of her women have an independent, almost mannish outlook on life, so the great majority of her men are womanish, some overtly homosexual. There is no great swingeing male animal anywhere in her fiction, and few women who give any sense of traditional feminine fragility and dependency.

That observation, perhaps I should say, is not made in reproach. Whatever the make-up of Mrs. Spark's characters, they always accord to logic, their own and the author's, and never neglect their primary obligation to the reader: to be interesting. The ironic title, *The Comforters*, would seem to refer to their blundering attempts to guide each other through the excruciating complexities of human relationship which Mrs. Spark understands so well. Here is Lawrence comforting Caroline over the voices which have been plaguing her: "When she stopped talking, he told her to hurry and get dressed. He kissed her as if she were a child." Four paragraphs later, he is himself struck with anxiety over his grandmother's affairs:

It seemed to Lawrence, then, that it was unsatisfactory for Caroline to be a child. He felt the need of her coordinating

mind to piece together the mysterious facts of his grandmother's life.

"You'll help me with my grandmother, won't you?" he
said.

The irony is unrelenting, but over and against it is a
curious kind of glee, that of the author revelling in her own
craft. Again and again, we get a sense of fun, of exquisite
playfulness, in the word-echoes and games, in the mind-
reading and the tangle of mystifications, which recalls the
best minds of the Renaissance testing their own strength,
or of Bryon teasing himself through sixteen cantos of *Don
Juan*. Nor is it just a question of style, but of actual
physical presence; although she has not allowed herself the
role of narrator, still she can't keep out of it. At one point
she bursts in thus, for all the world like Tallulah Bankhead
in *The Skin of Our Teeth:*

> It is not easy to dispense with Caroline Rose. At this point
> in the tale she is confined in a hospital bed, and no
> experience of hers ought to be allowed to intrude. Un-
> fortunately she slept restlessly. She never did sleep well.
> And during the hours of night, rather than ring for the
> nurse and a sedative, she preferred to savour her private
> wakefulness, a luxury heightened by the profound sleeping
> of seven other women in the public ward. When her leg
> was not too distracting, Caroline among the sleepers
> turned her mind to the art of the novel, wondering and
> cogitating, those long hours, and exerting an undue, un-
> reckoned, influence on the narrative from which she is
> supposed to be absent for a time. (p. 154)

And then, shortly afterwards, she intrudes this bit of madness: Caroline is explaining to a friend that the mysterious
voice—that of Mrs. Spark herself, presumably—which has
dogged all her previous actions has left her in peace at the
hospital.

> "The reason is that the author doesn't know how to de-
> scribe a hospital ward. This interlude in my life is not part
> of the book in consequence." It was by making exasperat-

ing remarks like this that Caroline Rose continued to interfere with the book. (p. 180)

This glory in the book itself, this intoxication with the immediate act of creation, a kind of artist's madness akin to the narcissism of young motherhood, is even more pronounced at the opening of her second novel, *Robinson*. This is the story of the castaways upon that curious man-shaped island—an island shaped like a man, that is to say. Here Mrs. Spark has her ideal laboratory, a beautifully prepared field, stretched out like Gulliver's handkerchief for the exercise of Lilliputians. Of course all the early books are Swiftian, not so much by design, one supposes, as by congeniality of temperament. Which does one enjoy more, the wit of *Gulliver's Travels*, or its author's ingenuity in providing occasion for it? Mrs. Spark is, in *Robinson*, still preoccupied—almost intoxicated—with writing itself.

The persona, January Marlowe, takes up the narration this time: in fact the book can be said properly to begin when she starts her journal. Once again the persona is writing the book. January is attractive, unmarried (a widow) and a convert to Catholicism. Once again, too, one of the principal men—Robinson himself—is a lapsed Catholic; it was the lover Lawrence in *The Comforters*. Robinson, who gives the man-shaped island its name ("no man is an island," somebody says), looks at first to be strong and self-possessed, but his resources are insufficient, and he has to fake his own murder in order to run away. The other men are Jimmy Waterford, amiable but weak, and Tom Wells, crude, foolish and larcenous—both recurrent personality-combinations in the novels. Villainy is associated once more with religiosity, although there is no one present whom Mrs. Spark can bring herself to hate as much as Mrs. Georgina Hogg of *The Comforters*. Never since Mrs. Hogg has she invested so much distaste in one character—a further illustration of the value of the first

novel as a campaign-plan. Mrs. Hogg and her paler counter-
parts, I think, represent the sensitive convert's extreme fear
of being misunderstood.

One other theme of prominence should be mentioned:
the war between privacy and loneliness. Many of us vacil-
late from time to time between a desire for the first and a
fear of the second, but the conflict is particularly notice-
able in the sort of person who so often figures in these
novels and stories. These high-strung, intelligent, unmarried men and women can't stand too much company, but
they are too neurotic to stay alone for long. And here they
are crammed onto an island! The situation is perfect for
those complexities which Mrs. Spark loves to explore, and
she makes the most of it. *Robinson* need not apologize in
the company of *Lord of The Flies*, *Robinson Crusoe*, or
The Tempest.

Her next book, however, surpasses it; indeed it is thus far
the peak of her achievement, and as such surpasses, it
seems to me, most of the books of our time. *Memento
Mori* is simply a masterpiece; the culmination of the early
trends which I have been cataloguing, and the perfect
wedding of her wit and irony with her sense of the fantastic. The plot is nothing, merely the elbowings and shov-
ings of a lot of superannuated Englishmen and English-
women. They shuffle along in the dim reaches of their lives
much as they have always done, cheating, lusting, black-
mailing, pestering each other for precedence; but they are
finding it increasingly difficult to hold their own: "The
teapot was too heavy for his quivering fingers and fell from
them on to its side, while a leafy brown sea spread from the
open lid over the tablecloth and on to Godfrey's trousers."
The mixture of pathos and absurdity which the book
presents is perfect. And the irony, too, has reached its full
potential: it is applicable to the whole human condition.

Whitney Balliett, in a *New Yorker* review in which he
called the book "flawless," identified its characters as a

"superb collection of grotesques." So they are, but what a lot more. Here Mrs. Spark has succeeded in presenting, not only her favorite types, but a cross-section of the whole range of human personality, including for example a really masculine man, although, significantly, in decay—the retired policeman Henry Mortimer—and a really man-centered woman, although significantly in charge since her husband's coronary—Emmaline Mortimer, his wife. There is the wise, watchful persona again, the slightly detached Jean Jaylor, formerly a lady's companion and now bed-ridden in a comic horror of a geriatric ward. There is her former mistress, the famous novelist Charmian Colston, struggling to keep her wits about her, and her husband, Godfrey, pitiful hoarder of sex-sensations and tea-cakes; and his sister Dame Lettie, fussy and fat. All these and more: critics, criminals, converts, Catholics—Jean Taylor is one, by conversion. It becomes apparent after awhile that these scarecrows are all the book has to offer—and it is then we realize that we are not watching grotesques, but people—ourselves. Our faults, after all, transcend our years. "Old men will become babes again"—these characters are all as sloppy and spoiled as so many infants, a point made directly by the sly interjection of a two-year-old near the end of the novel: "She gave the child his mug of milk which he clutched in both hands and drank noisily, his eyes bright above the rim, darting here and there."

The point is that we are with Swift again on his travels: Gulliver among the antediluvians, or visiting the floating island of Gerontia. The feeble lusts of Godfrey Colston, the cracked ego-mongering of the poet Percy Mannering, the mindless bullying of the dowager Tempest Sidebot-tome: they are all pointed out to the visitors to this absurd land. Local color—they are part of the landscape of old age. Like Gulliver, we observe the natives and we make our judgment: they are a collection of grotesques. But some-day the telephone will ring for us, too, as it does for everyone in *Memento Mori,* and the voice will say, "remember that you must die." The choicest irony is that which comes last.

Muriel Spark's next novel, *The Ballad of Peckham Rye,* is both a departure and a disappointment. There is no doubt that the line of thought which had carried her through her first three novels had worked its way to its logical conclusion in *Memento Mori.* And it is true too that anything coming just after that achievement would have to suffer by comparison. Nevertheless *The Ballad,* which relates the adventures of the demonic Scot, Dougal Douglas—I believe the name traces to the Celtic word for darkness—is more chaotic and incoherent than her best work. The difficulty is that her playfulness and love of mystification for once get beyond the reach of her Augustan diffidence and restraint. And so this novel or anti-novel, which celebrates as in the manner of a border ballad the coming of Dougal Douglas among decent folk, and the resulting smash of all their foolish ambitions, is a bit too hard to follow. Mrs. Spark has withdrawn her wise persona, leaving Dougal alone on the field; and thus while the resultant book is well worth the reading, it is not charged with the particular excitement that characterizes the earlier novels.

Also at the end of the fifties there appeared Mrs. Spark's first book of stories, *The Go-Away Bird.* Of these one may generalize that the longer they are, the better. She does not have the sort of mind that gives off little flashes of insight, occasional and perfect like the glints of a jewelled hand. She needs room, not much but enough for coincidences to sprout, for slow booming absurdities, for gradual ironies to blossom forth uncrowded. About two hundred pages is perfect, but she can make do with less. The very short stories are clever, but merely clever—one-shot absurdities of flying saucers and spirits, to make us blink and doubt our senses, but not to think. They are good but not satisfying. "The Go-Away Bird" itself, of which I have already spoken, is an excellent piece, just over fifty pages long. There are two others here of top quality, both mysteries: "The Black Madonna" (twenty-seven pages), in which a childless couple pray to a black statue, and get—but surely there is no need to say what; and "The Portobello Road" (thirty pages), a cracking good ghost story.

In *The Bachelors*, which Evelyn Waugh prefers to all of her other works, we are told, Mrs. Spark continues her efforts to get along without her persona, but this time much more successfully. She solves the problem, I think, by attributing certain of the feminine virtues of that useful character to practically all the men upon whose lives the book is based. If we run down the list, we can see how uniformly this is true: Ronald Bridges, the most sympathetic of the bachelors—all these men are by definition unmarried—sensitive, intelligent, agonizing, unstable, flawed—an epileptic—a Catholic who wanted to become a priest. He can have no lasting relationship with a woman, and is afraid of settling into a fussy and lonesome middle-age: " 'I'm becoming a prying old maid,' he said to himself." Ewart Thornton, "that big sane grammar-school master": a gossip (". . . avid, in an old woman's way, for her downfall," p. 148), a fussbudget ("a solicitous mother," p. 50), and actually woman-shaped ("his hips were wide for a man," p. 150). Reverend T. W. Socket, a pervert. Martin Bowles, successful barrister and mother's-boy of thirty-five. Mike Garland, transvestite. Matthew Finch, so guilty about his carnal appetites that he eats onions to repel the girl. (It doesn't work.) Patrick Seton, one of the focal points in the story, for it is his trial for forgery and false conversion that connects all the others. His is a more subtle case. He is a Don Juan, with a corresponding deep-seated hatred of women. Much of the tension of the beautifully constructed plot comes from the reader's knowledge that if he gets off, he intends to murder his pregnant girl-friend.

Not a particularly pretty group, and there are more like them in the book. Like the grotesques of *Memento Mori*, however, they have their relevance to those who judge them, and like the old people, they have moments of dignity and insight. One of these is devoted to one of Mrs. Spark's favorite themes, privacy vs. loneliness, by a futile small fellow, one Eccie Eccles:

> "You see," he was saying, "we are all fundamentally looking at each other and talking across the street from windows of different buildings which look similar from the outside. You don't know what my building is like inside and I don't know what yours is like. You probably think my house is comfortably furnished with its music room and libraries, like yours. But it isn't. My house is a laboratory with test tubes, capillaries and—what do you call them?—Bunsen burners. My house contains a hospital ward, my house—"

Here he is superbly undercut by a blundering question from Ronald Bridges, who having innocently wandered up, supposes that Eccie is speaking of a real house, thus ironically giving his support to the metaphor. *The Bachelors* is a fine book, but it too lacks, it seems to me, the best insight which Mrs. Spark is capable of, that which she gains from posing her special kind of woman against her special kind of realism.

For that reason I was delighted with her next book, a novel of the very finest caliber, and almost exclusively female. Mrs. Spark closes her accounts with men, for some time at least, with *The Bachelors*. In *Memento Mori* a certain phrase appears often: "laid to rest in their prime," p. 18; "They were both past their prime," p. 72; "nearing the end of your prime," p. 105. From this recurrent snatch of words, perhaps, was born the idea for *The Prime of Miss Jean Brodie*, the most subtle, and with *Memento Mori*, the most beautifully reasoned of her novels. Miss Jean

Brodie is of course the Spark persona, rushing back into the vacuum with double energy. As she is the most detailed recreation of this character, so she is the most memorable figure, up to this point, in Mrs. Spark's fiction.

Jean Brodie is vigorous, independent, a feminist, beautiful with a strange beauty, unmarried and, for once, a protestant. Her religion, however, is an error of birth which she has not corrected by conversion: "she was by temperament suited only to the Roman Catholic Church; possibly it could have embraced, even while it disciplined, her soaring and divine spirit, it might even have normalized her." She is no longer young, but "in her prime." This is her favorite phrase; it resounds through the novel like a battle cry. And it is war between Miss Brodie, unorthodox teacher in a conservative girls' school, and all the colleagues and conventions which surround her. On her side she has an indomitable spirit and a little group of disciples, one of whom, the novel's anti-heroine, or alter-heroine, finally betrays her to the authorities, so that she is dismissed. This girl, Sandy Stranger, after absorbing all of Miss Brodie's art, denies her and finally becomes a nun.

In this book Mrs. Spark experiments more broadly than before with chronology; we are constantly in motion from the present to the past and back, very successfully, too, for the human relationships with which the novel deals are tremendously subtle. Miss Brodie, for example, is involved with two men, one of them a painter, Teddy Lloyd. Among her other dispositions, she has arranged for one of her pupils to be his mistress:

> "I am his Muse," said Miss Brodie. "But I have renounced his love in order to dedicate my prime to the young girls in my care. I am his Muse but Rose shall take my place."

Much to Miss Brodie's displeasure, it is not Rose but Sandy who becomes Teddy's mistress. Yet all of Teddy's portraits, even those of Sandy, continue to look like Miss Brodie. Meanwhile Miss Brodie rebukes Sandy:

"Rose was suitable. Rose has instinct but no insight."

Teddy Lloyd continued reproducing Jean Brodie in his paintings. "You have instinct," Sandy told him, "but no insight, or you would see that the woman isn't to be taken seriously."

The Spark method is particularly suitable to the relationship between Miss Brodie and her girls. She has renounced her lover for them; abandoned marriage, in other words, for a covertly Lesbian relationship, as Sandy herself observes: "And Sandy thought, too, the woman is an unconscious Lesbian." (p. 176). So Miss Brodie fragments herself, disperses herself into her students who gradually draw away. She is betrayed and dismissed. Her prime is past. Sandy, her most intelligent girl, "insight but no instinct," has taken the most from her. It is their relationship, gradually quickening into a duel, that makes the book go. If a duel, it is a one-sided one, for Miss Brodie knows nothing about it. But her last year in the world is Sandy's, too. Miss Brodie dies of "an internal growth"—Sandy, perhaps?—and Miss Stranger enters the convent.

Surely the conflict which gives the book its special character, so enigmatic, so wryly amusing and yet profound, is that of Mrs. Spark's own life. The excitement infused into all her best fiction, that duality which I attempted to define at the outset, derives from some formidable positive charge of Edinburgh Calvinism against its opposite, the negative of mystical Catholicism. It is not safe to assign these functions blandly, in this novel or elsewhere: Miss Brodie, for example, though she resists Catholicism, is a visionary and an admirer of other strong systems, fascism, for one; and Sandy, the eventual Catholic recluse, is in many ways more hard-headed and perceptive than her teacher. But many authors have on the pages of their books given play to opposed sides of their own natures: Mark Twain, for example, with Huckleberry Finn and Tom Sawyer. Miss Jean Brodie is Muriel Spark's clearest conception of herself to the present, and Sandy Stranger her best insight into her most dangerous and self-destructive tendencies.

Since this book, the most self-centered and thus the most Romantic of her works, Mrs. Spark has attempted nothing so ambitious. *The Prime of Miss Jean Brodie* was a brilliantly successful answer to her need to return to the early material, and the necessity of finding a new statement for it, but the effort to write it must have been a costly one. Mrs. Spark works very quickly, we are told; her books take an average of six weeks to complete. Even so, *The Girls of Slender Means,* her most recent novel, can have given her nothing like the trouble of *Miss Jean Brodie*. It is certainly much easier going for the reader, although it too has its complexities, which are considerably heightened by Mrs. Spark's most advanced experiments yet in the matter of chronology. Well under two hundred pages in length, it seems something of a backwash from the greater works which preceded it, like the short stories which are often called into being by the passage of a novel. Mrs. Spark also published just prior to *The Girls* her second book of stories, including some radio plays, all of them worthy objects, called *Voices At Play*. None of these works has upon it the marks of a decisive new turn in her art, or the culmination of an old one.

Voices At Play contributes some new mysteries, including a science-fiction fantasy, some pieces with an Austrian setting, and one remarkable story reminiscent of "The Go-Away Bird," called "Bang-bang You're Dead," which investigates further the inexplicable turns of fate so well presented in the earlier story. Both use an African setting. The science-fiction play "The Danger Zone," while spooky enough in places, is a bit too contrived to be taken seriously, but another play, "The Party Through the Wall" is much more original, both foolish and frightening in the best Spark manner.

The Girls of Slender Means is a fine misty account of a strange club for young unmarried working girls; it has all of its author's usual virtues but it marks time, probably on the way to some new achievement of unimagined complexity. Still it is funny, with a delightful recapitulation of the speech patterns of young women:

> Dorothy could emit, at any hour of the day or night, a waterfall of debutante chatter, which rightly gave the impression that on any occasion between talking, eating and sleeping, she did not think, except in terms of these phrase-ripples of hers: "Filthy lunch." "Thee most gorgeous wedding." "He actually raped her, she was amazed." "Ghastly film." "I'm desperately well, thanks, how are you?"

All of these chirpings and flutterings come to a stop with a stroke of doom in the latter pages, carefully prepared from the start. Mrs. Spark's irony remains on the watch.

There are them, as I see it, two high points to date in the output of this brilliant and unconventional writer. Each stands out from among works related to it but lesser in overall quality and effectiveness. *Momento Mori* is the more objective of the two, a Swiftian vision of the world which overshadows even such ingenious works as its predecessors *Robinson* and *The Comforters. The Prime of Miss Jean Brodie* restates the problems of these earlier books in somewhat more subjective terms. Here the Spark persona finds herself the absolute center of the novel. There is no indication, however, that these two books, fine as they are, have succeeded in resolving what I believe to be the conflict that called them into being: the fundamental duality of Muriel Spark's worldview. There is in fact every reason to believe that Mrs. Spark's private war continues in unabated violence, and may shortly necessitate from her another gesture of dazzling virtuosity, perhaps this time a novel with an American setting. For unlike her great spiritual ancestor, she does not intend to stick pretty much to London, the British countryside, or to Bath. We are fortunate in this: if our time has brought forth new confusions, it has given us the writers to deal with them: new Jane Austens for new realities.

ANGUS WILSON:
THE TERRITORY BEHIND

Arthur Edelstein

> . . . and now I'm old; too old at any rate for what I see.
> Oh, I do see, at least; and more than you'd believe or I can
> express. It's too late. And it's as if the train had fairly waited
> at the station for me without my having had the gumption
> to know it was there. Now I hear its faint, receding whistle
> miles and miles down the line.

STRETHER'S FAMOUS LAMENT has found its contemporary
spokesman, appropriately, in Angus Wilson, a novelist
more clearly in the line of Henry James than perhaps
anyone else writing today. In *Anglo-Saxon Attitudes, The
Middle Age of Mrs. Eliot,* and *Late Call,* the best of his
five novels, Wilson has produced what amounts to a tril-
ogy on the theme of the wasted life, a theme he situates
on several intellectual and social levels. Although these
works are plainly concerned with the transfiguration of
British class structure in the twentieth century, the essential focus is always upon the solitary crisis of consciousness.
They are all late calls, these novels, centered in the twilight
awakenings of their aging and conscience-ravaged protagonists, each of whom opens his eyes belatedly upon his
past, to discover there not only waste but muffled horror
and devastation (evoked for the reader in recurrent images
of physical deformity: the crippled hand, the severed leg,
the grotesquely humped back). Unlike Strether, however,
who renounces the final happiness proffered by Maria

Gostrey, each of them once again takes up the reins of possibility. But in this act resides the bleak irony of their condition, for with the partial exception of Meg Eliot, who is not yet fifty (Wilson's protagonists are normally a good deal older), they have nowhere left to go. While it is not too late to learn how to live, it is in fact too late to live.

Though committed to the finest scruples of technique, Wilson is not an innovator—not, at least, in the sense that we would apply the term to, say, William Burroughs or Nathalie Sarraute. He does not test the possibilities of uniquely arranged syntax or of the free-floating consciousness. But like all serious novelists (including the best of the innovators), like Zola (a writer he is especially interested in), he experiments with the causes of a particular human predicament. Where he departs from Zola is in the delicacy of the experiment. For to the severely limited materials of the Frenchman's laboratory he has added the factor of consciousness as a vital influence upon his characters—and that makes all the difference. It is upon the minute, deliberate, accumulating apprehension of motives that the novels in large part rest. And this is appropriate to the advanced age of his characters. At a strategically situated point in their lives, that last chance to locate the right direction despite a tangle of wrong turns behind them, his people are put to the test of awareness. They must rediscover the lost past in order to confront the unfound future. Consequently, their movements ahead (their actions) are halting and confused, their return upon the past (their reflections) at once sweeping and meticulous.

Wilson's newest novel, *Late Call*, has the most substantially rendered central character he has yet produced and is in this sense his best book. Yet it is disappointing. And for these reasons it can serve better than any of the others as a gloss upon Wilson's treatment of the theme, for it illustrates his essential methods functioning at their best and

worst. The Wilson novel always incorporates a key circumstance of very high charge which serves to occasion not
only the actions and reflections of his protagonist but to
produce as well a thematic suggestiveness which will explain these. One of the imperatives of such a method is
that it not be overloaded, for if too much demand is made
upon the source of power it will—sooner or later—break
circuit. That is the case in *Late Call*.

In her sixties, Sylvia Calvert, a recently retired manager-
ess of small hotels, goes with her husband to live in the
home of their son Harold, a schoolmaster whose wife has
died a short time before. For half a century—a
lifetime—Sylvia has shuffled through the hallways of existence, avoiding the hazards of human contact. After a life
of hard work, order, and repression, she finds herself in the
progressive atmosphere of Carshall, one of the new towns
that are Britain's equivalent of exurbia. Surrounded, in the
ranch house of Harold and his three teen-age children, by
all the work-saving gadgetry of modern living, she is forced
despite her wishes into a life of indolence—forced for the
first time into communion with herself. But there is nothing to commune with. Her life is one enormous vacancy, a
blurred infinity of unlived years. Thrust mercilessly into
consciousness, she must reenter the flow of time—as the
symbolic touches of the narrative signify (she receives a
clock as a retirement gift and is besieged in the ranch
house by the dials of timing devices). When she seeks
narcosis in popular fiction, cheap biography, and the
"telly," she is thwarted by her fears and her sense of
worthlessness and becomes preoccupied with images of
violence. The world beyond her is a great darkness, an
enveloping atmosphere of decay and death, into which she
dare not venture, but which at the same time she cannot
evade—for it is within her too.

The contrasting personality of Arthur, her husband, is
instructive. Though he too has abdicated from life, he has

made his peace with this fact by continually re-creating for himself a fictional existence. Harking back to his experiences in "the great war," he tells heroic lies (and probably comes to believe them) which place him at the hub of sensational exploits. And he nibbles at the edges of other lives, absorbing something of their energy by constantly borrowing money he has no intention of repaying. A cluster of eccentricities, Arthur is a marvelously rendered character in the tradition of Dickens. Prone to sudden outbursts of temper (which are just as quickly forgotten), given to crude failures of restraint, Arthur serves as a gauge of Sylvia's repressions. To quell disturbance, to keep the surface calm, she secretly pays his debts, clucks at his lies, stills his tantrums and ignores—determinedly—his farts.

In two powerfully rendered incidents, the pivotal scenes of the novel, are shrouded both the explanation and resolution of Sylvia Calvert's smothered nature. One—the novel's prologue—occurs in her childhood, on the far side of that fifty-year gulf, the other in her old age. Both are terminations, both are beginnings. Without identifying her, the first shows Sylvia at the age of ten abandoning her chores on a hot summer day in 1911 to ramble through the woods with Myra, a little girl who is a paying guest on the rundown farm of Sylvia's parents. They shed their outer clothing, swim in a pond, and make floral wreaths. Though Sylvia thinks they are in a wood inhabited by gypsies, against whom her mother has warned her, they soon emerge, carrying their dresses, to find themselves behind the rectory, to realize they have merely been in a small grove of trees, and to be confronted by Myra's mother, Mrs. Longmore. Influenced by an innate Victorian prurience despite her progressive ideas about the handling of children, Mrs. Longmore mystifies and dismays Sylvia with half-veiled insinuations that something vulgar must have transpired among the trees. The shock of the incident might in itself explain Sylvia's lifelong repression (there are hints in later chapters that the adult Sylvia is disturbed by the slightest physical contact with women—and perhaps with men), but beyond that the scene evokes in its details the entire atmosphere of repression in which Sylvia's childhood was shrouded. Opening with emblems of abandon (woods, gypsies, the shedding of clothing), it concludes with tokens of constraint (the rectory, the grove mistaken for the full forest, the bedroom in which Sylvia is soon confined).

The novel's crucial scene, an extended variation of the childhood excursion, is embedded in the details of Sylvia's stay at Carshall. Urged to abandon the twisted and confining solace of her books and television by Harold's friend Sally Bulmer, Sylvia, though harried by a sense of rootlessness, begins to take solitary walks on the edge of town. (Again the details suggest a symbolic presence. Sally Bulmer is said to resemble vaguely a gypsy; during one of Harold's parties, Sylvia finds her alone—it is their first meeting—in the "leafy darkness" of a room decorated with ferns. Like those people of the undiscovered childhood forest, she betokens independence.) When Sylvia decides, despite her inordinate fears, to explore the uncultivated country beyond Carshall, all paths lead her back into town. Finally, however, she breaks from their restraint and makes her way into the woods, an act signifying her first faltering steps back into that emptiness where she must seek her being. Having slept through her history, she must reenter it awake, must return into the dream to find its meaning. And her initial success is implied when she encounters an old, hump-backed woman who tells her of a life spent wandering through the morass of war, upheaval, horror of twentieth-century Europe. Although the tale is distorted, hunched like the hag herself, it constitutes Sylvia's hazy first union with the past, with the convulsions of history through which she has sleep-walked. But like Sylvia, the hag too has hidden her face from the rampage of life (significantly, she and her husband had been dealers in *ostrich* feathers), living instead in her own desires and fears—which have congealed into a paranoid conviction that her children are attempting to poison her. In the old woman, who has dragged across the earth (like the senseless cargo upon her back) a burden of fear, evasion, and distortion, Sylvia has encountered a grotesque image of herself, a twisted reflection of her own obsession with death, and her own continued avoidance of the reality of her son and his children.

Subsequently, Sylvia meets the personification of a better alternative. When a storm breaks, she flees into an open field, fearing that lightning will strike the trees around her.

> It was only as the rain began to fall, swamping the world, that through its clatter she could hear a voice screaming. . . . Turning, she saw that where the field sloped away to her right, one tall crumbling, leafless, ghostly-fingered oak tree had been left to decline and fall in its lonely sovereignty over the landscape. There, clinging to the tree trunk, with face pressed close to the lichened wood, the little girl might have been guardian in a game of grandmother's steps, if it had not been for her hysterical, agonized yelling all on one high note of panic.

Overcoming her terror, Sylvia drags the girl to safety just before the tree is struck by lightning. In embracing the hysterical child "until they seemed to merge into one sodden mass," she unknowingly transcends that repressive fear, that sense of the body as sin, which was generated so long ago by her encounter with Mrs. Longmore. Returning across time to that early crisis in the woods, she has reentered, reenacted, and reversed it. Under the cleansing storm, she has at last fronted a hazard and dared an action. In the game referred to by the text, one child hides his eyes against a tree while others advance toward him. When he turns, they must hold their positions, however awkward, or be disqualified. Sylvia's life, an enormous frozen moment in a game of grandmother's steps, has begun again to stir.

The ensuing events in the little girl's home are laden with further suggestions of renewal. Having returned to that moment in childhood to emerge once again from the woods—to start over—she is treated this time like a heroine—and like a child. In that earlier time she had been beaten and sent to the isolation of her bed. This time when she is put to bed she is rewarded with sensual displays of affection: Amanda, the little girl, climbs into bed with her; Mrs. Egan, the mother, kisses her full on the lips. The entire occasion is an assault upon those Victorian barriers maintained for half a century. (That the Egans have come from Victoria, a place they hated, is in itself suggestive—and excessive. Wilson too often indulges in this kind of forced fussiness.) Since she has suffered a mild stroke in the storm, Sylvia is unable to control her speech effectively. But on the next day she has returned to normal, has learned, that is, to talk. And she soon begins to do so, hesitantly at first, by asserting herself and gradually taking part in the affairs of her family—by assuming an identity. It is under the continued influence of the Egans, shunners of pretense and formality, that she makes this transformation. And in responding to Amanda's persistent demands for accounts of her childhood, Sylvia resurrects her past—what there is of it—and reties the broken thread of her life. Wilson's strategy for placing the reader in the position of Sylvia is to orphan the prologue (the childhood scene), to let it fend for itself. Just as her origins have been lost to her, the prologue remains for the reader irrelevant, disconnected, and lost (he does not even know the identity of its central figure) until he seeks out the muted details which explain it and assimilate it to the novel.

And by overleaping that half-century, Wilson creates a further opportunity: to juxtapose two worlds, to deposit a product of pre-World War I Edwardian England in the context of post-World War II progressive England. The irony is that they are not really different, the two Englands. Harold, despite his modern home, his up-to-the-minute gadgets, his permissiveness in dealing with his children, and his progressive writing on education, is in truth as spiritually reactionary as Mrs. Longmore, the "progressive" mother of 1911. On the surface an advocate of life, he is fixed in the attitudes, or what he believes to have been the attitudes, of his dead wife. A partisan of local liberal causes, he is unable to take seriously his younger son's interest in the peace movement, seeing it as a childish eccentricity. The "understanding" letter he writes to his older son, on learning that the latter is a homosexual (it was evident all along, though not to Harold), is as futile and dishonest a gesture-after-the-fact as Mrs. Longmore's guilty present of a pink scarf to the little girl whose life she has blighted. When Ray, the older son, will not return and reform, Harold is determined to "wash [his] hands" of the "little whore."

Even his obsessive efforts to preserve the town's meadow against business interests that wish to erect a building on it signify his real though unconscious feelings. The open territory for which he fights is one surrounded by the town, tamed by it. In its very name Goodchild Meadow implies his attitude toward Ray. The "understanding" response is proffered only if Ray will be a good child, only if he will incorporate himself into the patterns of the community—otherwise Harold will show as little concern for him as for the open country beyond town, upon which the builders are also encroaching. Goodchild meadow is merely that small grove of trees which Sylvia had mistaken in 1911 for a gypsy wood that "might stretch on for ever" like the forests beyond Carshall. Harold is a blind victim of his own puritanical orthodoxies—and when he stages at the local school (with a sense of satisfaction, a sense of having gone into league with the young) a production of Osborne's "Look Back in Anger," he is solemnly unaware, as is everyone else, that the proper target for that angry look is himself. 1911 is 1964 is . . .

One has a special reaction to this novel, a feeling that a masterpiece has been allowed to slip away. That is, in a way, very high praise, and the book earns it—which is why it is so disappointing finally. Wilson, having produced a major character, fails his own creation through a clumsy evasiveness much like Harold's, a failure of the sensibility. For with the notable exception of Arthur, he has denied life to all the other characters. Consequently, one cannot take Sylvia's transformation seriously. The Egans, presumably the foremost agents of her change, are no more real, surely, than the creatures she must have seen on the "telly." And the younger Calverts are equally unconvincing. There is a sense of external manipulation in the motions of these people which is entirely absent from those of Sylvia and Arthur, the figures Wilson has thoroughly imagined. Though it is difficult to document this briefly, an example will perhaps be suggestive. When Wilson speaks through his puppets, he falls out of voice, and descends into cute formulas of expression which are meant to convey the tone of casual, homey talk. Shirley Egan calls her husband "Timbo" (Tim); Ray refers to people as "boyo," tells them they are on their "ownio"; the Calvert children respond to the anger of Harold by saying the letters "TFFTST" (time for father to stop talking); and so on. Although such devices may occur in real speech, the effect in print is a mannered, self-conscious dialogue—which in this case is frequently as mawkish in its substance.

The point, then, is that Wilson fails to populate Sylvia's world with figures who could generate the kind of pressure, the kind of convincing influence, which would justify so radical a change as the one she undergoes. As a result one is left with the uncomfortable sensation that the forest, the storm, the oak tree, the hag, and so on—the *symbols* of her experience—are the sole agents of that profound change. We have, then, an authentic character undergoing a metamorphosis provoked by its own metaphors. A real toad in an unimagined garden! To put it extravagantly, it is as though Huck Finn had responded not to his experiences along the river but to Trilling's essay. Myth and reality fail to merge. Though her battles are real, Sylvia Calvert does not change; the author makes believe she does. Toward the end she simply fades away, to be replaced by an impersonator.

Wilson has created a character who is superior to the fiction in which she has her being. Having chosen for the first time to deal with a protagonist who cannot articulate or even understand her own condition, he has succeeded in evoking—through meticulous characterization and powerful imagery—the texture of her consciousness. But he is thrall to his own success, as though the creature must sustain its creator. For whenever he fails to project the consciousness of his protagonist upon the ongoing business of the novel, there is so sharp a falling off as to leave the reader entirely unconcerned. Sylvia Calvert is an achievement of the first magnitude; *Late Call* is not.

The Middle Age of Mrs. Eliot and *Anglo-Saxon Attitudes* have neither matched this achievement nor miscarried so disappointingly. Like *Late Call*, each of these is concerned with a late crisis in the life of a character who thought he (she) had long ago made his compromise with existence. Meg Eliot is thrust by the sudden death of her husband from the protection of an elaborate shield of money, status, and activity, a shield meant to deflect precisely the kind of stroke she has now received. Like Sylvia Calvert, she must seek in childhood for the source of her deepest fears. And Gerald Middleton, an aging professor of history who has lapsed not only from the promise of a brilliant career but from control of his personal life as well, is stirred by the pressures of conscience to engage in a research that turns out to be the study of his own history.

The central images of *The Middle Age of Mrs. Eliot* are the garden and the desert: the place of safety, order, contemplation, and the place of threat, delusion, emptiness. One is Meg Eliot's solace; the other her fear. As affluent, busy, respected Mrs. Eliot, volunteer committee chairman of Aid for the Elderly, she sees in the lives of the indigent aged the void which she has fenced from her own, that void into which she imagines herself sliding whenever she is forced into inactivity. Looking down from a plane onto an actual desert, she identifies it with her fear:

> . . . as it went on, hour after hour of rock and of meaningless plateaux and of shelves marked by equally meaningless windblown tracks, of great white lakes that deceptively promised water but were only salt pans . . . she found herself lost in it, completely and absolutely bereft of all that made sense of her life, forsaken, and ready for annihilation.

Ironically, it is *because* of her attempts to erect a barricade against that emptiness, to wall it away, that she is thrown, in her new widowhood, into the world of her fear. For the life of expensive activity and possession has eaten away her husband's money. Without that, without him, she is no longer *Mrs.* Eliot—as she soon learns from the responses of others—but *Meg* Eliot, who cannot work on unpaid committees and need not be accorded the old deference.

In a kind of pendulum movement, the novel swings between the sensed alternatives of her world. Having been ejected from the formal garden of her life with Bill Eliot, onto the windblown tracks and salt pans of a bleak and indifferent environment for which she is entirely unprepared, Meg crumbles under the pressure of her placelessness and goes to recuperate in the quiescent atmosphere of her brother's horticultural nursery at Andredaswood. Once again she is in the protection of a garden—this time literally as well as figuratively. And in a significant sense Andredaswood is a nursery of the other kind too, for it is there that she returns to childhood. She has rejoined the companion of her earliest years, to replay their games, to reminisce and to grow into knowledge. After a long period of regeneration, she descends once again—this time voluntarily, this time prepared—into the turmoil of a world which she feels "won't be able to take me by surprise so easily again." She has learned that her nature, unlike her brother's (he is ascetic, self-sufficient, asexual), demands the higher velocity of the city and society and that if she remains at the nursery she will convert it into a place of exertion and conflict, destroying the tight calm of her brother's painstakingly created Eden.

There is in this novel no disengagement of stimulus from response, as there is in *Late Call*, no overburdening of the symbolic episodes. The therapeutic balm of her brother's insularity and the arboreal peace of the nursery provide the appropriate conditions for Meg Eliot's recuperation. And—this is important—it is simply that, not a transformation. The novel does not insist upon a metamorphosis and therefore has no need to justify one. What Meg Eliot has really learned is that she *cannot* change, that she is compulsively dependent on others in a way that causes her to cripple, to destroy them (as she did to her husband, as she had commenced to do to her brother), that if she is to avoid provoking catastrophes for herself and for others, she must live her own life and live it alone. A modern Eve, she has been privileged to return into the garden, but to her second exile from it she has added volition and the fulness of self-knowledge.

The major shortcoming of the novel is the protracted account of her degeneration and renewal. This is fiction by attrition, much in the manner of Dreiser's treatment of the decline of Hurstwood. But where Hurstwood's burden, the grey, lacerating, crushing solidity of the city, produced a mounting sense of pressure, Meg Eliot's more delicate circumstances and responses tend to dissipate the initial tension caused by the death of her husband (an event shrewdly contrived to take the reader unawares with the same stunning impact as Lieutenant Hearn's death in *The Naked and the Dead*). Although its details are carefully crafted, its important characters convincingly rendered, although it is sustained by appropriate imagery, the book is a tour de force with insufficient force. Its defects are not so striking as those of *Late Call*, but neither does it have the sturdiness of character presence and the strong projection of injured consciousness upon the landscape, which are to be found in the later work. The effectiveness of trial by nuance must always depend upon an intricacy and force of character that matches the urgency of circumstances — upon the sense that it all *matters*.

Anglo-Saxon Attitudes is still the most fully achieved novel Wilson has produced. While it has not the reach of *Late Call* either, its exploration of Gerald Middleton and the tangle of afflictions into which he has drifted is more scrupulous than anything we have been accustomed to since James. Wilson's remarkable attention to method can be seen most strikingly in the pervasive thematic and functional influence of the book's focal event: the discovery in 1912 of the tomb of Bishop Eorpwald, a seventh-century Christian convert. Suitably, since Wilson is probing the bygone seasons of his protagonist's life, that event antedates the time span of the novel and exists in the far background. But like James's Mrs. Newsome, who never appears in the pages of *The Ambassadors*, it is a looming and potent spectre in the foreground.

To begin with, Eorpwald's tomb has been the cause of Middleton's early lapse from the vigorous pursuit of his career. That a pagan idol discovered in it may have been a hoax has shaken his faith not only in the noted scholar who directed the excavation but in the entire discipline of historical research (ironic, since the idol has been taken as evidence of Eorpwald's default from *his* faith). The tomb, moreover, is at the hub of his long-delayed search into the truth about the idol—and, by extension, into the nature of truth entire. Like the quest of Oedipus, that search for an answer leads him to lay bare all the terrors and devastations of his own existence and to unearth the knowledge of his complicity. He is led back to those private evasions, long forgotten, long discounted, which have nevertheless swept across the terrain of his life, blighting and contaminating—breaking his marriage, alienating his children, decaying his initiative.

Aside from its function as an element of the plot, the Eorpwald excavation is a perfect effigy of Middleton's circumstances. Like his formerly inert consciousness, the tomb has enclosed the past in its darkness and has hidden those broken and decayed artifacts which can be disinterred only by digging beneath the level surface of the present. In his wife, Inge, Middleton too has trafficked with a pagan idol. And just as he did too little, and that too late, about the questionable object in the tomb, he has done too little about the idol in his own life. Both deceptions have been allowed to run their destructive course through time.

In a context which exploits medieval history as one of its materials, it is no accident that Wilson has made Inge a Dane (though perhaps the suggestiveness of this fact relies too heavily upon the reader's memory for historical detail). For it was from Denmark that great waves of pagan invaders—carrying with them their idols—came to assault and occupy England between the time of Eorpwald's death in the seventh century and his reburial in the tenth. And suggestively, Middleton's marriage to Inge was caused, indirectly, by the same Gilbert Stokesay who per-

petrated the Eorpwald deception, since Middleton married her in reaction to being spurned by the woman he
wanted, a woman who had decided to marry Gilbert.
Middleton, whose chosen life is ostensibly dedicated to the
pursuit of reality, has incorporated into that life a being
distinctly incapable of seeing reality, a silly, sentimen-
talizing woman who dwells in a "world of indulgent sweetness and syrupy intimacy." She is able to wink even her
responsibility for the terrible maiming of her daughter's
hand, able, in fact, to sentimentalize that disfigurement
into a cause for cheery, doll-house solicitudes.

Wilson strikes a nice balance in the portrait of Inge
Middleton, creating a being who is ruinously blind to the
wrenched realities around her, who actually nourishes herself on the catastrophes she refuses to see, but who is
nevertheless sympathetic. And he involves her in scenes
that are similarly balanced: painful and comic. Inge presid-
ing over a Christmas celebration at the local school:

> . . . Mrs. Middleton called up a very angel-pretty little
> boy of six from the audience—there was nothing she liked
> more than angelic faces in children—"And now little
> Maurice Gardner will sing a verse of 'Holy Night' and we
> shall sing the choruses. Little Maurice is a very shy,
> special little boy," she said to the audience, "so we must
> all help him."
> When no sound came from his terror-struck mouth, she
> bent down from the heavens above and placing her huge
> doll's face close to his, she asked, "What is the matter,
> Maurice? Have the trolls bewitched your tongue" so creat-
> ing a deep psychic trauma that was to cause him to be
> court-martialled for cowardice many years later in World
> War III.

This passage illustrates, too, the way Wilson sounds muted
echoes of his key incident, of his theme, in even the most
minute details of the novel. Amid a ritual celebrating the
birth of Christ, Inge ingenuously descends "from the heav-
ens above" to confront the "angel-pretty" Maurice with

her own "doll's face" and her Germanic pagan creatures. A troll has indeed bewitched his tongue!

The paradox of Middleton's efforts, his late but uncompromising researches into truth, is that they show his life to have been as deep a lie as Inge's. When he at last holds up to the faces of his family the terrible deformities he has discovered in *their* lives, hoping that *they*, at least, may see and avoid the consequences, they reject his interference. And it *is* interference. He is too late. The consequences are already happening. By unearthing the facts, he has simply alienated himself more deeply.

Like all investigations into the heart of the matter, into the foundations of truth, *Anglo-Saxon Attitudes* is inconclusive—but suggestive. To hint at the implications, one must overstate: reality, since it is not fixed, demands scrutiny instant by instant. The fact cannot be confronted *after* the fact, for by then the evasion is also a fact, irrevocable and often desolating in its consequences. To seek out the past in the hope of erasing that evasion is an exercise in futility and frustration. Whether Eorpwald thirteen hundred years ago, whether Inge thirty years ago, fell into apostacy and error, these are dead issues. What Inge does today, Middleton tomorrow, these are what matter. That Middleton in this moment looks without evasion into the next, this is what matters. Only the living instant can be conciliated. And this awareness is all that the past can contribute to the present. But it is everything.

In these works Wilson has produced a triangular study in the dynamics of evasion. It is entirely fitting that the retreat into quiescence of Middleton, the man of intellect, should be a product of disillusionment—which is to say, a conscious decision; that Meg Eliot, half aware of her motives, threatened by the remembered insecurity of childhood, dedicated to the uses of property, money, and power, should plunge instead into activities over which she has a sense of control; that Sylvia Calvert, simple, passive, weighted by shame and a sense of worthlessness, should drown in a life of simple and ritual activity, activity which controls *her*—and thus abolishes her. (She erases the sin by erasing the sinner.) Although, by virtue of his high awareness, Middleton is moment by moment the most interesting of the three, he is compounded—since Wilson cannot equal James's command of thought as action—of too many mechanical impositions, too many collisions of consciousness and plot; in short, too many coincidences of perception. It is Sylvia Calvert, at the other end of awareness, who, though she abridges (like Huck Finn) the opportunity for complex renditions of thought, provides Wilson with the challenge of the essential creative act, the evocation of that sense of life, of presence, that is the signal of an achieved character.

It is evident in Wilson's work that he is a writer of the highest seriousness. His concern with that journey into the darkest recesses of the self is one which has inhabited all of literature. It is the passage of Oedipus, Gawain, Hamlet, Marlow, Raskalnikov. These comparisons are not meant to imply, however, that Wilson is of the stature of say Dostoevski or Conrad. It is easy to fall into the error of overpraising one's subject in order to justify it. Wilson has not yet made an achievement that would place him in the ranks of these great writers. Too much in his work violates the requisite set forth by James: that a fiction must before all things be interesting. Too frequently the vacancy and drag, the deadly friction, of the failed lives which are his subject take command of his work. As in the case of James, however (and it would be sheer sentimentality to say that James always fulfills his own requisite), the very frictions against which he works are a measure of his ambition, of the task he has set for himself. More and more he has renounced the easy targets so vulnerable to heavy satire and concerned himself with the nuances and gradations of human fallibility, those accretions that grain by grain build not to the sudden and sensational shock but to that atmosphere of muted terror that is most pervasively true to human existence—the terror of felt hopelessness, the terror of that jungle of evasions which can finally trap a life inescapably in its senseless grip. Wilson has gone a long way toward accomplishing his task.

NOTES

Kriegel—Iris Murdoch: Everybody Through the Looking-Glass

1. George Whiteside, "The Novels of Iris Murdoch," *Critique*, VII (Spring, 1964), 27.
2. *Ibid.*, 46.

Shapiro—Widmerpool and "The Music of Time"

1. Anthony Powell, *A Dance to the Music of Time* (New York, Vol. I, 1962; Vol. II, 1964). Vol. I contains *A Question of Upbringing*, *A Buyer's Market*, and *The Acceptance World*. Vol. II contains *At Lady Molly's*, *Casanova's Chinese Restaurant*, and *The Kindly Ones*. The seventh book in the series is *The Valley of Bones* (London, 1964). Subsequent references are to these editions.
2. These novels are *Afternoon Men*, *Venusberg*, *From a View to a Death*, *Agents and Patients*, and *What's Become of Waring*.
3. Frank Kermode, *Puzzles and Epiphanies* (New York, 1962), p. 127.
4. Powell, *A Question of Upbringing*, p. 2.
5. *Ibid.*
6. *Ibid.*, pp. 3–4.
7. *Ibid.*, p. 11.
8. *Ibid.*, p. 52.
9. *Ibid.*, p. 119.
10. *Ibid.*, p. 134.
11. *Ibid.*, p. 135.
12. *Ibid.*, p. 207.
13. Powell, *A Buyer's World*, p. 29.
14. *Ibid.*, p. 30.
15. *Ibid.*, pp. 70–72.
16. Powell, *At Lady Molly's*, pp. 230–36.
17. Frederick R. Karl, *The Contemporary English Novel*, (New York, 1962), p. 238.

18. Powell, *The Kindly Ones*, p. 107.
19. *Ibid.*, p. 127.
20. *Ibid.*, p. 133.
21. *Ibid.*, p. 134.
22. *The Valley of Bones*, p. 47.
23. *Ibid.*, p. 108.
24. *Ibid.*, p. 238.
25. *Ibid.*, p. 239.
26. *Ibid.*, p. 241.